FROM GUMSHOE TO

CYBER SLEUTH

BY

DEBBRA MACDONALD AND

JOYCE FOY

Look for these upcoming books by

Debbra Macdonald:

Nonfiction with Joyce Foy:

Blitz Your Book to a Best Seller 21st Century

Fiction:

Under the Christmas Tree

Tarred, Feathered, and Dead

Written Off

A Wolf in a Sheep's Cloak

FROM GUMSHOE TO

CYBER SLEUTH

BY

DEBBRA MACDONALD

AND

JOYCE FOY

Trade Paperback

@Copyright 2015 Debbra Macdonald and Joyce Foy

Library of Congress: #1-2598186291

Requests for information should be addressed to:

A Vegas Publisher, LLC.

284C E. Lake Mead Parkway, #262

Henderson, NV 89015

www.avegaspublisher.com

avegaspublisher@yahoo.com

First edition: 2015

Cover Design: Tugboat Design

ISBN: 0996843701

Printed in the United States of America

DEDICATION

This book is intended to inform, educate, and entertain those with numerous interests. There are those who've always wanted to be a PI, or some wanting to know the "how" of it to be successful. It's all there – you just need to know how to find it.

We not only provide the basic how-to, we share life experiences that enhance your visual recall of instances where such cases maybe related.

Good luck everyone.

ACKNOWLEGEMENTS

Many thanks for all the opportunities that we have had over our combined 60+ years of experience as female Private Eyes from both sides of the border: United States and Canada. We have been blessed with many real experiences on cases that have provided great insight to assist Investigators worldwide.

It has been a wonderful journey and through our collaboration, that we are happy to share an efficient, educational, and entertaining North American guide for Private Eyes on both borders.

It's a great tool box whether you are an investigator or want to be one. We are thankful for all the clients that required our unique services, for the ever growing field of Private Eyes evolving into web-based investigators, for our bosses that had to listen to us when we were overwhelmed with excitement and adrenaline as we caught a subject in action, for our fellow colleagues that inspired, guided, and provided the foundation of our careers so many years ago, and to all the bad guys, thank you.

Let the learning journey begin for the private investigator in you!

INTRODUCTION

What is an investigator?

Wikipedia, defines a private investigator

as…"often abbreviated to PI, private detective or

informally as a private eye, is a person who can be

hired by individuals or groups to undertake

investigatory law or legal services. Private

detectives/investigators often work in the following

capacities:

- Law firms in civil and litigation
  matters

- Insurance companies to investigate
  suspicious claims

- Members of the public for domestic
  cases including custody and divorce

- Business owners or corporations requiring due diligence, employment screening, and integrity checks

The investigator's assets include patience and perseverance, adaptability and resourcefulness, alertness and perception, have good memory and exercise good judgment, be extremely organized, and be able to write a concise and 100% accurate report that can be easily understood absent of bias or opinion. "Just the facts, Ma'am."

Other assets include the ability to conduct surveillance without causing harm to himself, herself or others, define an investigation plan of action, and execute it quickly while the case is fresh in everyone's mind and documents and scenes haven't been altered or changed. Having the proper investigation equipment is also critical to a successful career.

This book doesn't contain everything you need to know to be a private investigator –no book can do that. But the basics are here. Follow your nose.

If you don't have common sense – this isn't the career for you. It takes an innate ability to think on your feet during times of great pressure, while avoiding bad choices that could cost you or someone else their lives, careers, reputations, and/or marriages.

TABLE OF CONTENTS

Accidental Death Claims

The accidental death benefit provision of the life policy (formerly known as the double indemnity provision) is essentially an accident insurance. Thus, the usual limitations closely parallel those in accident policies. Be sure to read all the provisions as many change from year to year and carrier to carrier.

For example, many companies have inserted a restriction relating to death from "inhaling gas" because of the increased number of carbon monoxide deaths. A fairly typical provision in current contracts reads as follows:

"Upon receipt of due proof that the death of the insured occurred before the policy anniversary nearest his 65th *birthday in consequence of the accidental drowning or bodily injury effected*

15

solely through external violent and accidental means, which injury is evidenced by a visible contusion or wound on the exterior of the body, or is revealed by an autopsy and that death occurred within 90 days after the date of such injury and as a direct result thereof, independently of any other cause and provided that the policy and this agreement are then in full force, the company subject to the conditions herein set forth will pay an additional or accumulated surplus in the same manner as the face amount unless otherwise stipulated.

This agreement shall not cover death resulting directly or indirectly from any of the following causes:

- *Self-destruction- whether the insured was sane or insane*

- *Homicide – any violation of the law by the insured*

- *Military or naval service in the time of war or any work thereto*

- *Any aerial or submarine activity (Exception: it does not include activity as a fare-paying passenger in a regularly scheduled commercial airline.)*

- *The taking of any kind of poison or the inhaling of any kind of gas or any bodily or mental disease or infirmity or bacterial infection other than infection occurring simultaneously with and in consequence of a bodily injury*

The company shall have the right and opportunity to examine the body and make an autopsy unless prohibited by law."

One common misunderstanding is that this provision includes an exclusion for drinking. Although driving while intoxicated is a violation of law and would be pertinent to the part of the provision that reads "any violation of law by the insured," it still remains fairly common among limited accident policies.

Guidelines for Handling:

The following is a suggested step-by-step format given only as a universal guide. Never hesitate to use your common sense, ingenuity, and imagination.

Interviewing the Claimant:

In a high percentage of cases, this first step can be omitted from the accidental death claim investigation if the customer provides you with the authorizations to obtain medical records. Otherwise, you might interview the Claimant in much the same fashion as that for the contestable death claim.

Completely explore the circumstances leading up to and surrounding the death. Obtain as much detailed information as possible, including exact dates and times, locations, witnesses, and the activities of the deceased just prior to the incident.

Coroner:

Frequently, this is the first contact on an accidental death claim investigation and in all cases should be made early in the investigation. It is difficult to outline a procedure for obtaining information from this source, because of the wide variation in the qualifications and procedures followed by these public officials both in Canada and the United States.

As a general rule, coroners are required to investigate every death caused by accident and all deaths that occur without a physician in attendance. Their methods and procedures in investigating these deaths vary by area and individual. However, major cities now have competent medical examiners, qualified investigators, and coroners on staff.

The ideal procedure is to personally interview the local coroner, but an acceptable substitute is a review of the complete report at the office of the Provincial Chief Coroners in Canada or the Coroner's Office or Medical Examiner in every city and town in the United States. Unfortunately, in today's environment, they're very busy people, so if you have remaining questions, ask them but understand that it may take time to get the answers you require, especially in larger cities like Los Angeles, Chicago (that experiences double digit body counts almost every weekend and more on holidays), New York City, and Miami.

Their office will also include toxicology reports, but it isn't necessary to see the autopsy photos unless it's part of your assignment. Final anatomical diagnosis is generally sufficient.

Police Records:

A copy should be obtained. It's rare that a department will not release one to you for a small photocopy fee. Both Canada and the United States have Freedom of Information Acts that allows you to obtain the documents legally and in a timely manner.

Witnesses:

Witnesses are normally disclosed through previous contact with Claimant, coroner or police records. In large cities, it is generally unacceptable to take any witness statements from the coroner or police officer.

Witness statements should be obtained directly in smaller cities or when accidental death is in question and on the more important cases. In Canada, the appropriate section of the Accidental Death Claim Questionnaire, Form #1459, should be used as a guide when interviewing a witness (es). In the U.S., the witness information is usually redacted (to protect their anonymity.) Develop a friendly relationship with a police officer in the record's department that will, at least, provide you that person's information – verbally and off the record. Then do your own interview.

Other sources:

Depending upon the investigator's findings, consider these items:

- Contact Medical (physicians and hospitals).

- Employer may be a source for decedent's usual activities.

- Newspaper accounts and photos of the scene also provide additional contact leads.

- Neighborhood sources may be the only source of new leads.

- Observation of the scene of the accident is especially important on cases involving falls or jumps from any heights.
- Photo(s) of scene is/are important.
- Other interested insurance companies should be considered for job related deaths connected with automobile accidents or workers' compensation.

Aircraft Claims

Background

Wilbur and Orville Wright have the distinction of having the first recorded plane crash on September 17, 1908 when a propeller fell off the plane, and Orville tried to land safely, but failed. Both he and his passenger were seriously injured.

Planes are designed to rise into the air, fly and land safely. Crashes today occur by pilot error, plane malfunction, and by terrorists.

Most aircraft deaths are accidents, violent and unexpected, leaving considerable wounds and/or sometimes death. Why then do customers request accidental death claims involving aircraft accidents? The reason generally has to do with some specific policy provisions offered by the insurance carrier.

Some policies exclude the additional accidental death benefit with wording similar to this ... *"When death results from operating in or descending from any kind of aircraft on which the insured was a pilot, officer, or crew member, or in which the insured was giving or receiving any kind of training or instruction."*

Instead of exclusion, some policy provisions make a positive statement to cover when the additional accidental death benefit will be paid like this ... *"When on a regularly scheduled flight in a commercial aircraft, as a fare-paying customer."*

The intent of both approaches is generally to restrict the additional accidental death benefit to those situations whereby the insured is merely a passenger on the aircraft and not in any way connected with the actual flying of the aircraft.

Some policies include a "non-occupational" section that rules out the additional death benefit when the death is a "job-related" accident.

The investigator must have not only a copy of the policy, but instructions from the company supervisor as to the company's position on the exclusion or benefits.

Therefore, the investigator's first step will be to determine if the insured was only a passenger or if he/she was involved in flying the aircraft, or if the flight was related to the insured's occupation.

Your client's assignment will include such questions as:

- What was the insured's exact status on the plane at the time of crash?

- What were his/her exact duties, if any, on the flight?

- Was insured giving or receiving flight instructions?

- Was the purpose of the flight business or pleasure?

- What was insured's destination? Why? Was flight plan filed?

- What was type of plane? Dual control?

- Who owned plane?

- What was position of bodies when found?

- Any recorded conversation with control tower?

- Did insured have any type of pilot's license?

- How was insured identified?
  (Sometimes the remains are difficult
  to identify).

- Do you know of anyone who took
  photographs? You'll need those.

- Have you been contacted by any other
  professional for information? Get that
  contact info and follow up and
  determine their purpose for
  involvement in the accident and/or
  client.

Sources of Information

Clients or counsel might include specific
handling instructions from specific sources. In
Canada, it's Air Transportation Canada ("ATC"), a
division of Transport Canada ("TC"). In the United

States, it's the National Transportation and Safety Board (the "NTSB") of the Federal Aviation Administration (the "FAA"). Clients may also provide the personal information release form or original policy signed by the target, next of kin or the insurer to permit the investigator to obtain all documentation from these sources.

The TSB – Transportation Safety Board of Canada, Air Investigation Branch, completes a thorough investigation of every air accident in Canada. The Air Investigation Branch has experts that assess the data recorder better known as the black box. The three stages of investigation include: the Field Phase, the Post-Field Phase, and the Report Production Phase. In Canada, stringent privacy laws require that the investigator submit the necessary forms for disclosure. Often the details of the case are released in findings on the government website.

The NTSB of the FAA completes a thorough investigation of every air accident occurring in the United States. Branch offices are located in all of the larger cities. The status of the investigation, plus limited information, is usually available at the branch office locations. While they may not divulge the exact cause, they can often provide leads that the investigator might pursue.

For example, people involved in the accident, where it happened, type of aircraft, owner, what local authorities investigated, where flight originated, names and addresses of witnesses, names of those first on the scene, etc.

In Canada, Air Transportation Canada outlines the various sanctions and rules surrounding aircraft carriers. The TSB official records are made available through their office in Greater Halifax, Nova Scotia, if the records requested fall under the *Canadian Transportation Accident Investigation and Safety Board Act* of 1989. The TSB and *Access to Information and Privacy Acts* are applicable to retrieve the findings.

Once the investigator has met the burden of all Acts, then the request can be submitted to the Transportation Safety Board of Canada. The thorough investigation and findings through this body of the government on the federal level will be posted under the section of Proactive Disclosure for public viewing categorized under the year of the accident. This is a great resource for investigators that are locating previous losses of a particular air carrier.

The reports will not be available until the findings are complete. It may take several months to have the Freedom of Information coordinator grant the investigator access to the documents requested. Often it is faster for the client to order the documents first hand and provide them to the investigator for further examinations and analysis.

In the United States, official records are available only through the Washington D.C. office of the NTSB. If a customer requests a copy or the investigator deems it important, the request should be referred to Washington. The official report is often delayed, sometimes by several months, but a partial report is usually available right away. The delay is often due to the fact that many independent resources report to the NTSB. They might include the coroner's report, toxicology results, local police reports, the insurance investigator assigned to the accident by the carrier like United States Aviation Insurance Group (USAIG), witnesses, metallurgy tests, and other experts.

Interviewing the Claimant (Beneficiary):

An interview may not be required, depending on other leads and the amount of information the investigator already has gathered. Where an interview is required, the following information should be obtained from the claimant or beneficiary about the deceased referred to as the insured:

- Why was the insured on the plane?
- Did the insured have a pilot's license?

- Did insured own the plane?

- What type plane was involved?

- For whom did insured work?

- What were the exact circumstances of the accident - date, time, location; etc.?

- Any witnesses? Who accompanied the deceased to airport? Who saw the deceased take off?

- Who was on the flight with the deceased?

- Who notified the Claimant (beneficiary) of the incident?

- What were insured's activities prior to the incident?

- What was the purpose of the deceased's trip? Business or pleasure, or both?

- Had the insured ever traveled to this location in the past? How frequent, when, and with whom?

- Past health, even if not contestable, may be a factor to be explored briefly.

It is important to realize that the beneficiary may be grieving, so a gentle soft approach by the investigator is required. Do your homework first through the Internet and online databases so there are no surprises during this interview. This will shape the investigator's questions.

For example, if there was a public article where the wife was charged with assault against her late husband six months earlier, you may want to be prepared for this. Furthermore, it may prove insight into the logistics of the relationship between the beneficiary (Claimant) and her late husband.

Social media and open source intelligence may also provide insight into the relationship and identify other family members or friends that could be interviewed if further information was needed to verify the claimant's statements.

Medical Examiner or Coroner:

Always obtain a copy of their report and ask for copies of any photographs taken at the scene. The report will reveal how the body was positively identified. The autopsy may reveal prior health conditions. They may also identify other investigators or authorities working on the case.

First Response Investigators or Detectives:

Police who investigated at the scene of the accident would be the next logical contact. This might be a local police department, a sheriff, a fire department, etc. Investigators should keep in mind that these authorities are usually on the scene only for two purposes: To offer life-saving services or to determine if a crime was committed. They can also provide additional leads, such as identity of witnesses, photographs, and diagrams of the scene while intact, etc. A copy of the pilot's log is also critical to the investigation.

Use of Internet:

Google Maps and Map Quest have a number of features that could assist in Arial photographs of the area in which the accident may have occurred.

This map could also be honed by month and year. This could prove important to show the actual location on the date of loss. It will also identify other businesses and residences in the general area. This may assist with potential witnesses and video documentation that may assist in the investigation.

First Witnesses on the Scene:

Witnesses would most logically be contacted when there is some question as to whether the insured was flying the plane or not. The question of the position of those in or near the plane should be explored carefully with such witnesses.

News media is another excellent source of information. The media will have photos and most likely video of the accident scene. Obtain a copy of any film available as well as interviews of witnesses at the scene that will spontaneously provide information you cannot get anywhere else.

Survivors:

Survivors, (if any) could know whether insured was flying the aircraft and helps to determine if the flight's purpose was business or pleasure.

Employer:

The deceased's employer can also confirm the flight's purpose. If the insured was self-employed, associates, secretaries, business calendar, and websites could also confirm details of his work activities.

Airport Authority:

The airport operator, fixed base operators, air traffic controllers in the U.S. or NAV Canada may have had contact with the plane. They could know who was piloting the plane. Important questions:

- Was flight plan filed? By whom? What conversations were held between the control tower and the plane? Was insured a pilot or just a passenger? Was the pilot was coherent and clear when making contact with the authority?

- Owner of the plane could describe the insured's connection with the flight (pilot or not), explain who was pilot if not the insured, the purpose of the flight, and the identity of the liability carrier.

- Anyone that accompanied insured to the airport should be contacted to confirm that the insured boarded the plane (especially important if identity is in doubt). Can anyone also possibly explain purpose of the flight and insured's involvement?

- If training flight involved, flight instructor should be contacted to confirm that the flight was a training flight.

- Liability carrier of the airplane should be considered, although customer is usually interested primarily in the cause; therefore, this source is not necessarily a good one for providing information the investigator is interested in.

Other Circumstances the Investigator May Encounter

Occasionally, an investigator may encounter some of the following points:

- Did the insured have a pilot's license? If any doubt, consider utilizing the Ottawa office if the flight involved a Canadian carrier. The FAA in the U.S. issues all licenses.

- Possibility of suicide exists. If so, the motive section of an accidental death questionnaire should be followed.

- Case is also contestable. If so, investigator should also follow the contestable death claim instructions.

- If the aircraft and/or deceased has not yet been located, investigation should

be concentrated on the Claimant
(beneficiary), the airport where flight
originated and possibly the employer.

Other investigation tools include:

1.   Obtain all service records on the plane's
maintenance.

- Obtain the pilot's log.
- Review pilot's history of flying.
- Obtain copies of the medical
  examinations that cleared pilot for
  license.
- Review the plane's manufacturing
  history for potential recall issues.
- Obtain the history of ownership of the
  plane and what work might have been
  done – get maintenance records.

- Conduct an area canvas and pick up all the film shot by local and area witnesses and professionals, i.e. police crime scene experts and newspaper photographers.

There are many resources and witness interviews that may be conducted if there appear to be red flags in the initial investigation. These concerns should be reported to the client in your findings with recommendation for further investigations. Instructions will be provided if the client believes it is required to mitigate the file.

Asset Recovery and Searches

In the past, investigative tools included old fashioned footwork, knocking on doors, having a "deep throat" in places like the police department, banks (in North America and overseas as well), credit unions, and other money industries to identify assets.

Today's technology leaves little room for hiding assets unless the person involved is very, very sophisticated. Even foreign banks give up names of the clients if you have the right contacts. Firstly, identify every possible name under which the person could have hidden the asset.

Obviously, the wife's maiden name or her middle name is most commonly used. Variations on spellings sometimes are used. Purposefully misspelling works. Try all the family names including the children and distant relatives including mother's maiden name.

Conduct the following searches:

- Find properties, vehicles, and general assets to recover.

- Find sources of income.

- Find the place of residence for service.

- Prepare the evidence and report for service.

- Service of the documents and affidavit.

- A preliminary investigation would be very similar to this type of case.

For finding sources of income or financials– it helps if you have a contact in the banking industry. Sometimes, all you need is a name, social insurance/security number, and state of residence to identify all the money being held in every bank in the United States in that person's name.

One U.S. investigator had a deep throat in the banking industry that only needed a name. The informant, for $300.00, could locate all monies in all financial institutions around the world—not just the banks.

In today's economy, asset recovery and searches have increased due to the loss of income, foreclosures, divorces, family-children kidnapping, skip-tracing, and high rates of unemployment. It's easy to identify details of property registered in the subject's name, utilities in their names, and other identifying information.

Locating a car or house allows the creditor to repossess or place a lien on the property or execute a judgment. Take photos of the property to demonstrate its existence. Also, verify any numbers such as serial or model numbers.

This enables a process server to deliver the documents and produce an affidavit to the courts. Or to assist the repossession company in identifying the property, albeit a car, truck, boat, plane, etc.

Serving summons or repossessing property are both very interesting jobs and require a lot of common sense, clever ideas, and working outside the box. It's not unusual to take a large bouquet of flowers to the door. Use any ruse you can. It's also a good idea to be able to RUN FAST, as sometimes an investigator needs to make a quick exit when a situation doesn't go as planned.

In Canada, the privacy laws permit limited access to information unless there is a breach in contract of law or the client has a signed release form. An investigator can still access some public information that enables them to track down liens, property ownership, and civil litigations that offer insight to the targets' whereabouts. Where there is a signed release form from the subject, more information can be obtained publicly to locate their assets.

The information highway is swarmed with people publicly donating their personal information. Social media has come to the forefront and often provides details of employment, residency, and marital status. Individuals openly display photographs of themselves at the cottage, in their boat or new sports car. These are all tools that need to be followed up to close your file. A work-up sheet of those sites to check may yield you the information to locate assets from afar.

The history of one's past criminal record is not available in Canada; therefore, when serving summons or statement of claims to targets, investigators are often without knowledge of previous violent history. So, if the information highway does not identify the subject as an offender then there is no way to be prepared for this. In any event, investigators should take a self-defense course to insure they are able to protect themselves in certain circumstances. Be alert when serving such documents, and if looks like it is going to go badly, it probably will. Stay in shape for a better chance of running if necessary to get away safely. See a pattern developing here? Get in shape!

An investigator is considered the same as the general public with no permission or authority to carry a weapon or firearm throughout the Provinces of Canada. There are few exceptions to this rule that require a special order of the Supreme Court of Canada.

In many American states, one must complete a background check, be vetted by the FBI, take a firearm written and shooting test, and be fingerprinted and photographed by the local police department in order to obtain a Concealed Handgun Permit. Each license is renewed every so often where the gun owner must repeat all these steps again. That permit may or may not be reciprocated for every state the person carries it into. So, that person may be fined or even arrested if carrying a concealed weapon into those non-reciprocal states.

Background Investigations

People and companies conduct background checks for a number of new 21st century reasons that include pre-employment, pre-marital, and/or dating reasons. Preliminary searches include public social network websites, residential databases, and reverse look-up search engines, people searches, bankruptcy and lien searches. These searches are usually low cost and online. The White and Yellow Pages available on the Internet are quite valuable resources. Google Earth can also be used to actually see the property once a location is identified.

Searches are utilized through Facebook, LinkedIn, My Space and others, too many to mention. Where an account is found for your subject, be sure to print the profile, as it could be changed or even deleted prior to reporting the information.

Often these profiles provide photograph, date of birth, and city of origin, marital status, and family make-up. By far, the culture of 2015, and advanced technology has altered the investigative techniques of years past when neighborhood door-knocking took hours, if not days to complete.

Facebook depicted Mary Sue Doe as a pretty blond bombshell who was photographed drinking beer at Total Bar and Grill. Other pictures associated with her profile included a list of employers, college and high schools. She was married to John Doe and had three children. Photographs of her husband identified a red Voyager van as the family's mode of transportation. As investigators, it is necessary to dig deeper than just the profile that is displayed. Click on the friend's list, and on her husband's profile.

Leave no profile unturned. If the individual has not secured the profile, then it opens for viewing.

The Internet has opened many doors for an investigator; the available information through social networking is invaluable. Remember that everything you send into the Internet world never leaves. Even employers have resorted to checking those sites on prospective and current employees…be cautioned.

During a recent case, we located the subject's business profile as a self-employed sales representative for ABC Cosmetics. Our investigator printed the profile. The remainder of the searches were completed over the next twenty-one days and nearing a pre-trial. The investigator completed searches to insure that the findings were accurate. The subject no longer represented ABC Cosmetics. She had returned to her previous employer as a sales representative. Both documents were addressed and submitted in the final report.

In this case scenario (and all cases), it is most important to remember that an investigator should always print out, each and every article found in relation to the subject in case the information or situation changes prior to the report filing.

Public searches also provides details of the subject's address, association of liens registered in their names with others, including significant others and businesses. Be sure to review and copy the history of previous claims, losses, and faults through courthouse records. These also identify patterns of behavior and activities.

During a preliminary investigation with regard to money laundering through a medical clinic operated by the subject, a property search completed through a local land registry identified a

matrimonial lien on the property with a spouse that

did not have the same surname as the subject. All the

necessary documents on the purchase and mortgage

of this property were acquired. Next, the investigator

attended the local courthouse and conducted

searches under the subject and her spouse's name

through civil, family law, and small claims courts.

There was a family law matter before the courts that

identified the subject as respondent. A review of

these documents provided all the business

documentation for the subject and her business,

including the fact that she was able to deposit

$60,000.00 cash in the first month of her business

opening.

A paper trail can be relied upon as good evidence in a court of law. All documentation should be printed, dated, and entered into the report.

In-Depth Background Inquiries:

Subsequent to a preliminary investigation, an in-depth background may be warranted. This may also occur following surveillance, where the subject was either active or inactive.

In a situation where the subject is active, determine the pattern and purpose of the individual's activities. The subject may be visiting a number of locations for sales or developing new business. He or she may be purchasing items for renovations, pricing a new home or vehicle, or pricing new items in preparation for the windfall in anticipation of the outcome of his case.

Dated, documented data is critical in everything you do as an investigator. Your report should never reflect your personal opinion. Let the paper documentation, interviews, and inquiries reflect the facts in evidence.

Further inquiries might be conducted with previous employers or co-workers. In some cases, the information may not be available due to privacy issues in a state or province. In that case, there may be other ways to successfully obtain the information through co-workers.

In a case where the employee worked for the local telephone service and the human resources office refused to provide details of the subject's employment, the investigator attended the branch where the subject worked and conducted inquiries with fellow employees coming and going from the location. As an investigator, you need to be inventive without breaking any privacy, provincial, state, or federal laws.

Neighborhood inquiries may also be warranted in order to ascertain pre and post injuries, as well as activities. This is inclusive of a corporate situation as well as a bodily injury claim. The investigator would approach neighbors with a general questionnaire to insure that you are not providing the witnesses with personal details with regard to the subject. Stay within the privacy laws of your state or province. When conducting such inquiries, the investigator should identify themselves and be prepared to show proper identification if asked. Always ask neighbors to identify which neighbor has resided in the area for the longest time or those who may be home the most, so that you can find someone who may be able to provide useful information. There's always at least one person in the neighborhood that doesn't like your suspect. Find them!

Bylaw infringement investigations

And when you find that neighbor, these are some issues that are bound to arise:

- Noise complaints
- Barking or dangerous animals
- Vehicles being repaired or disabled in the driveway or garage
- General bylaw complaints
- Fence line disputes
- History of issues with previous neighbors that may have moved due to constant complaints

- Kids that don't get along

Often neighbors do not agree. There is usually one in each community that has to have their own way. They often project unfounded grief on others in the neighborhood and will absolutely complain about everything and anything. Sometimes, this causes rifts between neighbors and bylaw infractions are reported. Such cases could relate to noise, fence or tree disputes, parking, poor maintenance, and animals. The complainant may be well known by police and bylaw officers. Unfortunately, the accusations have to be defended by the neighbor to avoid fines and prove innocence. In such cases a private investigator may be hired to defend the accusations.

In such cases, you may be called upon to conduct a due diligence investigation on the complaining neighbor to establish if there has been any previous history of reports to by-laws and police directed to previous or present neighbors. This may include civil litigations searches, by-law research, as well as, neighborhood inquires.

The work should be concentrated on the contents of the complaint, but be alert to matters in the past that might contribute to patterns or habits. Who else knows what the witness knows or knows more? Find them!

The burden of proof will be based on the probability of the evidence. This evidence and report may be used by the client to file a civil suit against the pestering neighbor after the by-law infringement has been proven false. The police may also intercept further complaints by warning the complainant.

In some situations, an investigator may have to provide field testing for noise, photographs, video documentation, measurements, and scene re-construction. The investigator must insure that the proper equipment has been brought to obtain the optimal results. If the investigator does not have experience in these areas, an expert may be consulted to identify the best approach.

In one case, several years ago, an investigator was sent to a house to determine the noise level that had been reported in a complaint from a neighbor. This person was found to be a regular complainer of all activities in the neighborhood. She had caused some nearby residents so much stress, that many had sold and moved from the area. The noise complaint was made due to the sound of a piano being played. During the investigation, at three hour intervals, a train ran one block behind the house, causing the houses to shake slightly. This noise had to be louder than a piano playing.

The decibels were measured when the client played her piano from inside, outside the house, and from across the street. The decibels did not reach close to that of the train. The evidence was compelling and provided that the client was within the bylaws. The neighbors provided great insight to the complainant who was known for her mental issues, constant complaining, and outrageous behavior to control all neighbors' activities.

Cheating Spouse and Infidelity

"Cheaters" is the number one television show that publicizes one role for private investigators. The reality show depicts attractive female private investigators luring married men at bars. In some venues and cases, this may be considered entrapment. Important things to consider include:

- Surveillance – can be covert (hidden in a van for example) and/or overt (in the open but remaining anonymous), depending on your assignment.

- Identify the third party. (Don't make a mistake and film and chase the wrong twin. An investigator did that once.)

- Identify third party address and particulars.

- Obtain photographs and video documentation of activity.

- Provide a detailed report of findings.

Surveillance, in its infancy, was advertised with the use of a long lens camera and binoculars from a hole in the back of a van. Our vision includes someone wearing a trench coat and top hat. The PI would follow the cheating spouse into the smoke-filled bar where he meets his lover and be wired somewhere on his body for audio.

Today, the tools include 21st century wires and cameras from lapel pens, briefcases, eye-glasses, you name it – there's a product for it. A spy shop visit (and there's bound to be one in your town) will enlighten you as to the possibilities. Plus, today's cheating spouse is more sophisticated. Thus, this is the most difficult type of surveillance.

It is like a shadow hanging over their head, as they continue to cheat.

Usually in these matters of the heart, it's possible that the client doesn't really want to know, even though they have hired an investigator to confirm it with evidence. They may have instinctively suspected, yet the heart remains in denial.

Although many relationships still start in the workplace or through extracurricular activities, the Internet serves as a global way to meet people.

Now with advanced technology, the ability exists to catch a spouse through GPS, cellular calls, Internet surfing, and online dating profiles. And what a wonderful world it is. From Match.com, Lavalife, to Plenty of Fish, it is easy to put yourself out there on the Internet. The key is how to find those profiles and the alias that they use.

As a seasoned investigator, the client needs to identify the changes in the spouse's behavior that causes suspicion of an affair. As well, the client should scan the home computer and check the history of sites visited to determine if the other half has been visiting dating or porn sites. If there are peculiarities, then an investigation may be warranted.

In a more recent case, a very educated client contacted our office to request a background check on an individual who was met online. This client questioned a number of stories that the subject had provided. The profiles online depicted the pilot as a long time employee of an airline who flew throughout North America. Stationed in a border

town to Canada, the potential match provided his

license details on a LinkedIn account. Facebook,

My Space and LinkedIn all legitimized his identity.

There were three issues that concerned this client:

Although he had flown into town, he never wore his

uniform or invited her to his hotel, he refused to

provide his home address and telephone number,

and upon checking his alleged pilot license, it was

nonexistent.

Was he married? That would be the first

investigative thought. It was necessary to conduct

searches in the country where he lived. It was

evident from these searches that the potential spouse

was actually a hardened criminal who had been

convicted of carjacking in his native state. The

photographs and date of birth matched. If he or she

seems to be too good to be true, check them out! It could save you heartache, financial loss, and your life.

Child Custody

These are among the most difficult cases for the investigator. It pulls the heartstrings of most people. It's also a great way to get between a man and a gun (as in domestic cases). Be safe and be sure.

- Interviews and statements
- Surveillance to observe activities
- Neighborhood inquiries at previous addresses
- Civil litigation searches for previous patterns
- Court searches for any criminal activity
- Granny and Nanny cameras

Investigations are conducted much like others in every facet of your work: take statements, interview everyone that might have any special knowledge of the family dynamics and that includes schools and churches. Document everything you see, read, and hear, both the positive and negative, against what appears to be the offending party. This is fair and balanced reporting.

Conducting surveillance can also be done, especially in public places like the parks, zoo, shopping malls, etc. where the use of a visible camera might be totally overlooked by the parties.

Don't forget to go to previous neighborhoods for statements and interviews, especially those with children, at-home mothers, and seniors who are mostly home during the day and enjoy being outdoors.

Obviously, you want to conduct both civil, criminal, and background checks from all available resources. Somewhere in all that work, you're going to find a "best friend" who knows everything that isn't written down somewhere else, and their "worst enemy" who will tell you everything.

In such fragile situations, investigators must use kid gloves. Often clients are anxious and result oriented. Lawyers want the results now, especially when their heartbroken eager clients bug them. This will deflect the personal contact with the client and keep the information secure. In such cases, instructions should be provided by the lawyer in charge. The reports will go directly to the law firm that can provide copies to the client. In these cases, it is best to protect yourself from reprise from the other side. Family law is a very messy and emotional rollercoaster that need not be part of your investigation. Stay neutral and unaffected; keep your emotions out of this type of work.

Civil Litigation Searches

These searches used to be done by going to libraries and the courthouse and squinting through hours of index cards, large green-paged books, and microfiche. Investigators today are lucky to have the Internet and search engines to utilize, instead of the gumshoe practices that were relied upon in the past.

- Superior court searches for Civil litigation as Plaintiff or Defendant
- Family law searches for Applicant or Respondent
- Small claims searches for Applicant or Respondent
- Criminal Law searches for cases before the courts
- Federal searches for law suits

- Estate law for court cases dealing with wills

Don't forget to conduct those searches throughout the regional courthouse where the target or family lived, worked or originated in the United States and Canada. And remember to check all names they formerly used and places they previously worked. Women are difficult to locate because of name changes. Hispanics often use their mother's maiden name as their last name. Vietnamese citizens often have their surname shown first and given name last. Often second generation residents adopt American names like John instead of Giovanni. In recent months, there has been an overabundance of name changes recorded. Such name changes are listed in the *Canadian Gazette*.

In the U.S., if the name change is done in a court of law, those records are available under the Freedom of Information Act of 1984, unless the court orders the case sealed, in which case you'll need a court order signed by a sitting judge to open the seal. And you better have a great reason for the request. A large number of adoptee files are sealed and not available—ever.

Some name change documents can be found online at www.ask.com/name+change+records. Sometimes fees are charged; sometimes the information is free.

Initial searches may provide variations in the name of your target. The basic Internet searches on their address, telephone number and employment plus social networking sites may give you better insight.

In many of the courthouses in Canada, the records can be found on a computer access-based system with the capability of printing the events of each filing in the proceeding. It also provides the other party involved and the next court date. This could prove invaluable when the subject cannot be found and surveillance is required. The subject could be landed at his proper residential address. It also may provide a safe opportunity to serve a summons or subpoena.

Cold Cases

With the advent of "Cold Case Files" and other television shows, the importance of re-opening old cases has created a new opportunity to give peace and closure to family members. The police departments in many larger towns have a completely separate department now dedicated to cold cases.

- Usually a twenty-five-year-old or older case
- Timeline of events from years past
- Witness list to interview
- Search public libraries for neighbors at the time of the incident
- Search township/city records, on microfiche to locate witnesses or records

- Have printouts of each of the searches to refer to
- Track family members who may have heard the stories

Sometimes, the family has simply given up on law enforcement and may even offer a large reward to find their family member, and they engage a PI.

Obtaining copies of everything ever written about the case is of paramount interest from every resource available that we've already covered in this manual.

The family usually has a scrapbook of items or events for you to use. Interviewing the reporter may also reveal other evidence or clues from their notes that were never pursued by anyone in the case.

If the investigating police department will let you have records (it helps to have friends there), hopefully the reports won't be redacted, and you can run down witnesses and other parties to interview. You may also request the information through the Freedom of Information Act in Canada with a joint submission from the concerned parties. In the U.S., the FOIA Act of 1984 automatically makes that information available to you without involving any parties associated with the case.

Cold cases are like recreating someone's life. You think of calendars, canceled checks, credit card charges, phone bills, grocery receipts, utility bills, gasoline expenses, receipts, anything with a date and a location on it. Start a calendar of those important dates within about six months of their disappearance.

On one case, a suspect was being charged with capital murder in over seventy cases. The local police department had looked at the suspect's MO and dumped every open case with a similar MO they had at the time. The investigator was able to recreate a calendar of events and determined that the suspect was in Fort Worth attending a computer class when a fresh body was discovered almost 1,500 miles away in Orange County, California.

While that isn't a cold case; it stresses the importance of organization and detail to facts – and documenting every timeline you can.

In another case, a black man residing in rural Northern Ontario accidentally fell to death will working for Hydro cutting limbs from tree in a small town fifty years earlier. The family had not rested and continued to keep every record even though it was old and frail. They hired a private investigator to review all the details of his death, as they believed a driver moved the truck and ladder forward causing the man's wrongful death. The family never received the man's pension, and the police conducted no interview with the possibility of wrongful death. The family needed closure. The investigator had to go back in time. The children of the dead worker spoke of stories from this era. There was one time when their father came home tarred and feathered. These stories took the investigator to a different point in time. The twenty-four boxes of memorabilia enabled the investigator to walk back in time.

Unfortunately, due to the fifty-year time lapse, problems with witnesses became readily apparent. Most were in old age homes suffering from dementia and other mental and physical paralysis.

The interviews were long with no ability to keep them focused with the bits and pieces of the events of his death. There were a couple of children that remembered their fathers talking about his tragic death. The entire crew had been devastated at the time and, when questioned, spoke highly of their former co-worker. Although prejudice did exist heavily in this time, there was no evidence that could confirm a hate crime.

The investigator followed leads and found a couple of widows who remembered an insurance policy that covered the Hydro works. Although these widows searched, the documents were not found. A search at the archived town records office was conducted. Searches of concurrent years identified payments to an insurer prior to and after the death of this man. Documents supporting those insurance payments were photocopied. The family was entitled

to their father's coverage through the insurance

carrier. Can you imagine the interest after fifty

years of being denied? Follow the paper trail. Never

give up until every lead has been followed.

Confidentiality and the Client

Many types of clauses bind the investigator to confidentiality with the client. In the U.S., if a lawyer has provided you instructions, the transfer of the information from PI to lawyer is deemed confidential and not accessible other than by court order. The investigator's work is deemed to be part of the "attorney's work product," and therefore not available to any Third Party or discoverable in a court of law. An investigator can be found in contempt of court if that information does become public knowledge. So can the attorney. Protect yourself by maintaining confidentiality.

In Canada, clients including lawyers may request that a confidentiality contract be signed. This contract may include a number of other clauses on the specific guidelines and policies that the vendor (the PI) must adhered to. All these policies are within the Canadian laws. Sometimes clients consider the investigator as simply an agent of the client. Any information that has been collected for the client is owned by the client and cannot be disclosed to any third party. This includes the police or courts, as it is up to the client to decide who the information can be released to. Therefore, the investigator must maintain confidentiality in even the smallest details of that case.

It is a very small world that we live in. You could be discussing a case with an unknown individual at a party. When you disclose tidbits of your investigation and this person knows the family you investigated intimately, you have not only breached the contract, you will be sued by your client and employer. There is no doubt this person will return to your subject and tell them your story.

You have jeopardized the client, the integrity of your

firm, and the case itself. A professional should never

share details of cases with anyone.

Contestable and Accidental Death Claims

Occasionally, the investigator will encounter a case that can be both contestable and accidental. In those instances, the insurer may view contestability as a more important issue than that of the accidental nature of the death, because the issue becomes contestable on whether or not the policy is in force:

- The accidental death investigation if completed first with emphasis on past medical history

- When that investigation defines accidental or not, then the case becomes one of clarification of insurability

Possible Suicide

This case requires developing and reporting the most subtle or apparently insignificant information to the client, unless the deceased leaves a note or verbally indicates their intentions to others.

Death Claims on Infants

Infant deaths are handled much like others. If the loss is contestable and the child was less than two-years-old at the time of death, emphasis should be on hospital records at the time of birth and interview of the attending physician who delivered the child.

Group Death Claims

The key here, as in all work, is to understand and comply with the policy provisions and exclusions along with the instructions from your

client. On group contracts, the agreement is between

a group of people and the insurance company. The

covered individuals are called "subscribers." The

most commonly encountered group death claims are:

Accidental Death Claims:

The investigator follows the normal

procedure for handling an accidental death claim,

EXCEPT that no contact should be made with the

insured group unless this is specifically requested.

Eligibility investigations:

The investigator must identify when the

deceased entered into coverage and continued to be

an active participant in the group. The most frequently requested information includes:

- Was the decedent working the specified number of hours (usually thirty hours per week) on the date insured?

- Review the employer records: payroll, unemployment tax forms, withholding tax forms, time cards, interoffice memos, expense vouchers, officer's minutes, etc.

- Was the decedent actively and regularly working those required minimum hours from the date insured up to the date of death?

- Define specific job title, duties and/or income of the decedent.

- Was the decedent totally disabled from the date last worked until the date of death? Some policies provide death benefits.

Other group coverage:

In every case, identify any other group carrier at the time of death. That might include unions, fraternal organizations, and other similar units by:

- Check with neighbors.
- Follow up with the individual organization.
- Look at the decedent's vehicles and all others in their family for organization or parking lot stickers.

Insurability investigations:

These are only encountered occasionally and primarily under two different types of circumstances:

- Determine if the individual may be employed, but opt out of participating in the group coverage.
- If the person later agrees to be insured, he/she must present evidence of good health, attest to be in good health, submit to a medical examination, etc.
- A franchise group carrier may provide coverage.

Credit (Life) Insurance Death Claim:

The coverage may cover the life of a borrower of money or the purchaser of goods is insured in connection with a specific loan or credit transaction. Pre-existing health history prior to the date of issue alone is usually not a basis for denial of benefits. Most commonly encountered issues include:

- Was the individual actively employed on the date of issue?

- Claimant was not employed and health history is developed that determines the cause of death and/or occurred within a specific time frame from the date of the policy issuance.

Court Preparation and the PI

Although investigations do not always lead to the courtroom, it is important to realize that there is always that possibility. Yes, your report, methods of investigation, notes, and credibility may be challenged. With this in mind, throughout all stages of the investigation, proper documentation is important.

Questions may be asked like:

- When did you write these notes?
- Do you use a tape recorder while on the job?
- What was the weather like on January 1, 2012?

These questions are often made to trip you up or have your notes, tape recording, and documentation entered as evidence. Your employer will provide an outline of particular requirements for your notes and final report. There are standards in place such as name of subject, date, time, file number, the weather to start, followed by the PIs name, license number, and weather.

In court, the investigator should dress accordingly. A business suit would be appropriate along with proper grooming. Clean shaven or neatly trimmed beard provides the judge and jury with confidence in the testimony you provide.

Criminal Investigations

By now you're starting to see the repetitive pattern of investigating. It's locating important people, taking their statements, having a great camera (with a date and time showing on it), and exploring every detail and documenting and preserving all evidence.

- Locate witnesses, interview and take statements.

- Conduct background inquires to locate independent witnesses.

- Reconstruct time line of events.

- Obtain video documentation from crime scenes

- Obtain crime scene photographs and measurements.

- Reconstruct accident scene

- Analyze and provide evidence package.

A man under the influence rounded a steep curve on a remote highway in the Cascade Mountain range crossed the center line, and struck and killed a woman head-on. He would be criminally charged with capital murder. Financially, he had the minimum liability limits on his policy.

The woman's family hired an investigator who conducted all the preliminary work and also attended the scene with a professional accident reconstruction expert only to find – the county had the road blocked, had blown out half the mountain, and was straightening out the road! It seemed that wasn't the only accident at that exact point, and the county had been forewarned several times, including

one newspaper story about the dangerous curve.

The investigator was able to obtain and

preserve copies of film that the crime scene team

shot upon their approach to the accident

immediately after it occurred.

Although the original scene had been

completely destroyed, evidence remained. That

obviously opened the county's liability and deep

pocket exposure for the deceased's family.

Criminal investigations that range from the

wrongfully accused to the wrongfully convicted have

resulted in a North American nonprofit organization

created to assist those serious voids in cases from

alibi witnesses to DNA. The witnesses were not

interviewed, not all suspects were explored, and

tunnel vision may have set in. In many cases, the

lack of manpower hours in police departments causes a great problem with their ability to completely investigate the crime and follow up on possible leads. However, most departments mandate is politically and publicly driven to insure that crimes are solved and charges are laid.

Often when conducting a criminal investigation request from a lawyer, the entire disclosure must be reviewed. A site visit to the location where the crime allegedly occurred will assist to take photographs and see what they could have seen. Often a witness's recollections are vague and unreliable. The witness has no motive or intention to lie. It is clouded in the mind, and memories fade quickly in time. Therefore, the sooner an investigator can interview and obtain a statement from the witness, the better. The job then becomes keeping them focused on the facts in a chronological order. This is the toughest feat for an investigator. People always want to tell you the truth. Thoughts don't always reach their mouth in the order that they were observed. Insure that questions have been prepared prior to a witness account interview.

Previous movies show the detective interviewing the suspect. The suspect is not able to make eye contact and when asked about the crime, his eyes shift to the left and slightly down. Then there is the guy fidgeting who can't even look at the officer and is sweating profusely. The cop leaves the interview and says they got their man. People have adapted to these theories, and in 2015, the sophisticated criminal can even beat a lie detector test. Some modern medications can also fool the polygraph. To add to the mix, different cultural and beliefs have made it nearly impossible to detect a liar. Koreans, like much of the Asian communities, find it disrespectful to maintain eye contact. It is a matter of respect and not necessarily a lie.

The basis of a conviction weighs in a criminal case heavier than a civil matter. The judge or jury must be convinced without doubt that the accused is guilty. Therefore the burden of proof is much higher. Thus, the investigator must be well aware of the laws such as the criminal code, laws of evidence, and rules of statement accuracy that must be given freely by the witness without pressure.

As a criminal investigator, it is not their job to judge, only gather the facts and report them as is. Often, the pounding-the-pavement gumshoe is able to find the scent. Like a dog with a bone, following a scent until the trail ends.

A case that haunted many residents for years, when a young beautiful female was taken from her apartment and her body was recovered within a three-hour window on the side of the road 100 miles from her place. The victim's car was still at-large and news stations plastered the plate number to assist the police investigation. The likely suspect, of course, was her ex-boyfriend who had been seen on the balcony arguing with her in the afternoon. This was a familiar sound to the neighbors as the couple had a volatile relationship for several months leading up to this. Then there was silence.

The evidence definitely pointed in his direction although he protested his innocence. His lawyer sent an investigator on the fresh trail the following night. A site visit of the apartment building identified no cameras to prove or disprove his innocence. The interviewed neighbors identified the time of silence as 6 p.m. with no activity observed after this time on that fatal day.

The following night around six in the evening, the investigator returned to the area and pounded the pavement from local stores to gas stations within a mile radius of her apartment. After an hour with no leads, perseverance kicked in. The small no-name gas station clerk near the entrance to the highway had seen the victim's car. There was a tall black man driving with a female slumped over in the passenger seat. (Not at all fitting the description of the accused)

Ask the right questions! Did the man pay by credit card or debit? No, the guy paid cash. Do you have video cameras that record the pumps? Remember, in this day and age, cameras are everywhere with only one issue, the documentation is often retained for short periods of time unless the owner is aware of a significant incident. In this case, the timing was perfect as the tape would have been recorded over within in the next five days. The evidence was secured, and the wrongfully accused was released.

Physical evidence speaks volumes. It speaks for the dead and injured. The dead can cry out to you from the grave. If you enjoy different challenges and let the evidence speak to you, criminal investigations may be your true calling. Pound that pavement!

Death Claims

From the perspective of life and health, and customer reaction, handling death claim services plays an important bearing on an immediate outlay of monies on the part of clients. They often involve large sums and top management of the customer's firm reviews and approves the reports. Consequently, all claim investigators should be familiar with some background information, understand the specific policy and exclusions, and follow all company procedures and instructions. Remember, no "personal opinions" – it's all based on facts in evidence.

General Provisions of Contracts

It is impossible for an investigator to know the details of all insurance contracts, yet it is important to understand some general provisions that are a part of many contracts. Here are some examples of the typical wording you might find in policies:

Suicide:

"If the insured commits suicide within two years from the date of issue thereof, while sane or insane, the company will be liable only for an amount equal to the premiums paid in cash hereunder."

Misstatement of Age:

"If the age of the insured has been misstated, an amount payable thereunder shall be such amount as the premium paid would have purchased at the company's published rate in use for the correct age

at the date of this policy. Age will be admitted on

presentation of proof satisfactory to the company."

Reinstatement:

"Within a period of time after default in any

premium payment, if the policy has not been

surrendered, it may be reinstated upon evidence of

insurability that is satisfactory to the company. (In

the event of reinstatement, health history is usually

only pertinent from the date of lapse to the date of

reinstatement.) The relevant time period may vary

from two to five years depending on the provincial or

state legislation."

Incontestability:

"This policy shall be incontestable after it

has been in force during the lifetime of the insured

for a period of two years from its date of issue,

except for non-payment of premium."

Non-smoker Policies:

"A reduction in premiums is available with most insurance companies for applicants who have not used cigarettes, etc. for a specific period of time predating the application."

Preliminary Analysis - Request for Reports

The initial review and analysis of the policy itself, coupled with the client's instructions is the place to start. If you have any questions, a call to the client clears up any misunderstanding. Be sure they give you a complete copy of the policy that includes not only the benefits, but the exclusions and limits as well.

Contestable Death Claims

As indicated previously, most life insurance contracts include a provision that allows them to contest a claim anytime within one or two years of issue of the policy, in the event of intentional or unintentional misrepresentation or omission of facts on the application. In most cases, the only guide provided to you will be the date of issue. In this instance, work on the assumption that the decedent admitted no medical history or medical attention during the three-to-five year period prior to the issue of the contract. When the customer states that a specific exclusion is contained in the contract (Example: application showed past medical attention for high blood pressure and policy contained a rider to exclude all circulatory ailments), you should investigate with consent to view to developing

119

history other than that causing the rider on the policy.

The most important point on this type of investigation is to prove or disprove past medical history. In most cases, once this has been conclusively established and documented, your work is done. For example, if you contact the regular family physician and he/she provides a statement confirming a pre-existing medical history, it is normally not necessary to continue the investigation.

Guidelines for Handling

The following is a step-by-step procedure for handling a contestable death claim. This proposed format is given as a guideline only. Your client may issue you more specific activities.

Interviewing the Claimant:

It's important to clarify that the Claimant is the beneficiary or next-of-kin who has filed a claim for the proceeds of the policy. In writing reports, the decedent is referred to as the Insured. Occasionally, the insurance companies will send medical authorizations with the inquiry, making any contact with the family unnecessary. On important cases, you may decide to contact the family (even though authorizations have been provided) to obtain other leads.

In cases where authorizations are not provided, it is usually necessary to call on the surviving spouse or next-of-kin to obtain signatures on waivers. Such interviews must be handled with the utmost consideration. (CAUTION: If a solicitor/attorney has been retained to handle this particular insurance matter, discontinue interview with Claimant and contact the solicitor/attorney.)

Usually deep mourning marks the period between death and funeral, and a call by an investigator might be regarded as an unwelcome intrusion. The interview should be postponed until after the funeral in most cases. (Exception: Industrial life policies pose a slightly different problem in that sometimes the funeral is held up until the insurance is paid.)

In your first contact, be sure to offer your condolences and apologize for having to intrude upon their time of grieving, but information they may have is necessary to expedite a decision on behalf of their insurance claim. They will want to see your authorization first.

Do not, under any circumstances use any meeting with them to cross-examine the Claimant. Use questions instead that can be explained by the beneficiary, rather than simply "yes" or "no" responses. They need to vent their sorrow as well. Your job is to listen.

If you don't know the name of the family or attending physician, try to develop that as early as possible. In addition, you may develop other valuable leads:

- Names of all other attending physicians
- Places of hospital confinement
- Medical attention
- Ailments doctored with home remedies

- Drugstores where prescriptions were filled
- Previous injury claims through a motor vehicle or work-related accident
- Address history for neighborhood inquiries

Place and length of employment, duties, recent change of activities, plans of the decedent (such as possible retirement), usual hobbies, recreation, and former addresses, if pertinent, can also be elicited from the Claimant by diplomatic questioning.

In every case, the wise investigator leaves the door open for a re-contact with the Claimant even though no re-contact is made on a high percentage of cases.

Medical Contacts:

In most cases, the medical information is the second step. You now have an authorization to obtain medical records, where you will see the complete medical history with focus on any problems prior to the issuance of the policy, or proof there is no prior medical history.

Obtain a signed statement from the physician on all deaths. Most experienced claims examiners consider hospital records an invaluable source of additional leads. The theory that a person sick enough to go to the hospital is sick enough to be truthful is generally accepted. It must be kept in mind, however, that an intern or a resident physician has written information contained in a hospital record from the Claimant. And even though countersigned by the attending physician, it can be subject to some question in a future dispute.

This is why a higher value is placed on a physician's statement than on a hospital record by many examiners. The past medical history section of the hospital record is especially important on contestable death claim investigations.

The Employer:

The next most desirable source of information on a contestable death claim is the employer. The investigator should be aware that some information given to the employer by the employee was shared with an expectation of confidentiality. An authorization will be required to view and copy those records.

Also explore the possibility of previous group insurance claims, workers' compensation claims, and employee benefits that may provide definitive information. You might also identify names of close associates, such as immediate superiors or fellow workers who might have some knowledge that's pertinent to the investigation.

Neighborhood Sources:

Avoid contact with neighborhood sources on death claim investigations when possible. If you do need to go to the neighbors, question them in such a manner as to cause them to reveal a tip or lead concerning the death and the preceding illness. With this opening, proceed to develop past medical history, especially names of other doctors or hospitals.

Potential Sources

The number of potential sources on contestable death claims is unlimited, but the following outlines some of the more common sources and the reason for contact.

Coroner Records:

Seek Coroner records when the deceased had not received medical attention at or just prior to the time of death. When the decedent is not under a doctor's care at death, in the U.S. and Canada, an autopsy is generally ordered and performed.

Police Records:

Of particular interest on cases involving chronic alcoholism or drug addiction, they may also serve a useful purpose on other important cases, in filling in the background of the deceased.

Probate Court Records:

Those should be checked on any case involving mental health history.

Trade or Fraternal Organizations:

These are excellent sources of information from the group coverage carrier and might contain possible past claims and medical history.

Suicide Prevention Service:

Do you have a suicide prevention service in your area? If so, don't overlook this service on potential suicide cases.

Smoker vs. Non-smoker Investigation:

Some life insurance companies offer policies for non-smokers, usually at a discounted premium designed to attract the non-smoker. The discount varies but may be equal to 10% or 20% or more for the nonsmoker over the smoker for the same policy.

Those life companies offering these policies at a discount for the non-smoker need to verify whether or not an individual ever smoked and how long. These are good questions to ask:

- Did the insured smoke in the specific period prior to the date of insurance/issue?

- Was the insured a smoker on the date of application for insurance?

- What were his preferences and extent of the insured's smoking habits - cigarettes, cigar, and pipe?

- How often did he/she smoke?

- How many packs per day, etc.?

- Did the insured smoke marijuana or other drugs of any sort in the past?

When asked specifically by the insurance company to investigate the smoking history of a person on a contestable death claim, the following are considered to be the prime sources for documentation:

- Physician interview, with signed statement to include any notation about smoking habits from the physician's medical records

- Hospital records, with photocopy of history section showing any mention of smoking habits
- Signed statement from beneficiary Claimant, commenting upon any smoking habits of the decedent

Remember: This aspect of investigation is only applicable when the client specifically asks you to do so.

Due Diligence

The client is conducting research to determine whether or not to hire a potential employee, a high risk client, someone who needs security clearance of some nature (like carrying a weapon), a business proposition, and/or rent or lease an apartment or home.

- To verify the information provided as correct or incorrect

- To review Internet documents for press releases

- Check all social sites on the Internet – once it's on the web, it's there forever.

- Credit sources will confirm business status, payment schedules.

- Lien, property and civil lawsuit searches on directors

- Civil and criminal checks on the subject

An investigator was able to simply conduct Internet work to determine if the person a woman client met online was actually married. Photos speak a thousand words. When the client met with the prospective date, she was dressed to kill. When she sat down, her opening question was, "Do you have the permission slip?" He asked, "What slip?" She replied, "The one from your wife saying it's okay for you to date." It's a short ending – but a safe life.

Environmental Investigations

Here's where sights, smells, and sounds play a part in an environmental investigation. Smoke rising in the air, water with a green oily slick to it, smells of sulphur – it's all there for the education.

- Attend the location and obtain photographs.

- Obtain samples of environmental concern.

- Check for video footage that may be on site.

- Interview employees, witnesses and associates of the business.

- Conduct covert surveillance to determine current activities.

- Determine bylaws and infractions that relate to the concern.

- Find directors names, and establish any association with other companies.

- Identify the city, county, state, and federal departments responsible for protection of citizens.

- Get every report, photo and interview everyone associated with the project in question.

- Establish a timeline that might help to decide whether an insurance carrier from one event carries over into another carrier.

- Check for infractions, fines, and newspaper reports on any previous incidents. An excellent case at point was the BP spill in the Gulf of Mexico a few years ago. When compared to other oil companies, they

had been fined many more times than

the next nearest competitor. That's

public information if you just dig for

it.

Healthcare Fraud

Health care fraud, along with drug and medical fraud occurs when a company or an individual defrauds an insurer or government health care program.

In the United States, this may be Medicare or Medicaid and other federal healthcare programs.

Canada's universal health care system provides coverage from province to province for basic medical services.

In both the United States and Canada, private insurers or company insurance policies offer coverage, as well.

Estimated fraud in the health care industry cost the taxpayer has been estimated as $98 billion, roughly 10% of the annual Medicare and Medicaid and $272 billion across the board of the entire health care system in the United States. In Canada, the estimated between 2% to 10% of health care claims had an element of fraud, misuse or abuse. In 2014, the health care costs were expected to exceed $214.9 billion, so the estimated fraud could be estimated on the high end as $214.9 million from the public purse.

Regulated and Non-Regulated Health Care

Honest providers in the United States will always ask you for a photo ID to make sure they are providing the medical care to the insured person. Sometimes they will also ask the patient to sign a form in their medical file that shows the date and time of their appointment.

Providers

Health care providers can milk the system by billing more hours that actually worked and for services that were never completed. Regulated or non-regulated health care providers could abuse, or misuse their credentials. This can be reflected in clinics and with other service medical providers.

Clinics

Every industry has the good, the bad and the ugly. There is a tendency to be wary of clinics that are overbilling, abusing and misusing insurance coverage. It is an opportunist type of fraud, and may be defined as a service that has overbilled, not necessary and in some cases, never accessed by the insured.

In some suspicious cases, clinic inspections may be required and necessary to detect the fraud.

During the course of an investigation, the investigator attended a clinic to obtain full disclosure of an insured's attendance at the clinic

for treatment. When the investigator arrived, there

was a tray of business cards on the counter for

different clinic names. There was a female seated at

the reception desk typing into computer, as the PI

looked over the desk, there is was a message pad

with a law enforcement agency and telephone

number. Quickly memorizing the number, the Private

Investigator noted that the office was absent of

medical equipment, patients, and chiropractors or

massage therapist. Yet the printer was spitting out

invoices. This was identified as a Ghost Clinic.

These types of frauds can also occur in
service providers such as daycare, cleaners or
maintenance worker. False invoices are billed often
by relatives or friend of the insured. This can also be
identified in a ring of individuals who perfectly

organize and orchestrate the misuse, abuse and opportunist nature of this crime. The service was often never provided for the insured who may or may not be aware of the billing.

Medical Identity Fraud

Identity theft on the rise and issues of the protection of our personal information has caused an influx on medical identify fraud especially when it comes to those who have no coverage so they steal an individual's information to obtain care and defraud the insurers, government and other providers.

Medical Equipment Vendors

There are many examples of fraud related to medical equipment vendors that supply wheelchairs, scooters, walkers, beds, and other medical equipment. This may include shipping more of a product than ordered or reasonably needed, not providing patients credits for the return of equipment, "up-coding" a form of billing more for expensive items, double and false billing for a product, and forging documents that only doctors can sign for.

In these cases an investigator may be required to verify that the accuracy of the billing, the return of equipment and verification that the insured was aware of the doctor's prescription. These are red flags specifically tied to the supplier.

Whistleblowers and Fraud Deterrence

There have been a number of systems implemented to deter this type of fraud including coding systems, Whistleblowers that report anonymously with immunity, as well as, inspections and regulations to deter these types of fraud.

Incident Scenes

As the investigation develops, minute details may prove to be the key to the solution of the case. Review the value of all evidence, be observant, and identify all possible resources. Look up and around you. It's all there.

Protection of the Incident Scene:

The scene should be protected from the accidental or intentional intrusion of unauthorized persons. From interviews, you'll discover if any changes have been made. Indiscriminate handling of the objects on an incident scene may result in the destruction or contamination of evidence. It could even make it appear that someone other than the actual guilty party is at fault.

Preservation of the Incident Scene:

You are seldom first at a scene of an accident or crime. Thus, you must trust that the experts (police, CSI, coroners) have preserved them with diagrams, photos, video, etc. Other conditions (snow, rain, high winds, a fire or explosion) often alter evidence at a site as well. In the U.S., don't forget OSHA. They always make the scene of disasters, and their reports contain volumes of evidence and information.

Photographs:

Photographs of the scene should be made from all angles. Pay particular attention to the size and measurement of the items, to portray depth. That's why the police place a ruler near evidence. Use a wide angle lens or do a panoramic overlap of several photos depicting the entire scene. Place it near a small object for perspective.

Sketches:

A sketch should be as close to scale as possible or use something single, like a coin so the relationship to the evidence is clear and measurable. The following rules should be observed when sketching an incident scene:

- Measure the room, to sketch a proper and appropriate diagram.

- Date and time should be recorded on the drawing and in your notes.

- Entrances and exits should be identified.

- Sketch any furniture from the location that it was found in the room.

- Measurements should also be utilized in case a sketch to scale should be required in the future.

- Measure evidence in precise location of the room from walls to furniture to entrance, etc.

- Ensure that the sketch has accurate points of dimension, restricted areas and viewpoints from the various angles in the drawing. (Often Video)

Internet Information Gathering

With over 50% of the general population in Canada and around the world communicating through social media accounts accessing them multiply times a day on their cellular devices, the World Wide Web provides great insight at your fingertips.

Whether it be Facebook, Instagram, Twitter, LinkedIn, Askme, Foursquare, YouTube, Blogs or other social media sites directly related to culture or language, everyone is communicating in this quick and remote manner. The World Wide Web has made it easier for investigators, insurers, and the general public to obtain a wealth of information at the tip of their fingers without even leaving their offices or homes. Incredibly, many users choose to share it openly without utilizing the strict privacy settings that social media sites have implemented and offer.

151

The Millennial generation utilizes their accounts over six times as day, and with this group, the percentage is substantially higher than the reported 50% of users. The social media and open source intelligence will be an invaluable tool moving forward for Private Investigators or Detectives.

Evidence Based or is it – Explore the possibilities

The provided profiles, posts, blogs, and ads are not fully verifiable as the content is submitted by the authors which could be the individual that you are investigating. The information can be used as a tool to conduct surveillance, establish leads for interviews, provide insight into a person's activities, lifestyle and provide photographic evidence to assist in all avenues of investigations. It can help you identify friends, relatives, groups and interests. This type of research has become the foundation and starting point in the 21st century investigator.

As the search parameters and websites change continuously, it is important to hone your searches to provide successful results. A name could yield you a million names and consume a lot of time. One easy way to find specific results is to use "quotation marks" with the name of the individual provided in the quotation. If the name is "John Smith" search results will be too vast, so you may want to add a city, state or province after the name. The more specific you can provide the search engine, the more relative the search results will be.

Discover the easiest way to enable the search engine to provide you with the most accurate and relative information. Also asking a question, provides honed results to fit your investigation requirements.

It is important as an investigator to realize that there are a number of variations when it comes to searching the World Wide Web (WWW). If the person is twenty-years-old, surely they have been introduced to the web at an earlier age and raised on the online foundation of social media. However, it is also important to realize that many people aged 60 and over are using social media to find old friends, keep in touch with relatives, and may be active online. So although we cannot conclude that someone may be active or not by the age group, the younger generation has more outlets to post their pictures, news and activities such as Instagram, done right from their smart phone.

Popular Sites:

- Facebook, Twitter, Instagram, LinkedIn, Askme, Foursquare, YouTube

- Residential databases, reverse look ups and relationships to the subject

- Google alerts, google profiles, maps, trends and images

- Blogs, web crawler, web pages, IP addresses, Kijiji, Craigslist, group associations

- Dig deeper into the web to find relationships around the world and leading social media sites in various countries

- Use key terms to find the information and a tool box of services for quick results

Just a note to all investigators: Google has a wonderful tool for tracking any publications on the

World Wide Web with your name or your subject's name that will send you an instant message with the article, blog or site daily when it is loaded on to the web. Utilize it when you can, as you never know if a related article, posting or blog may be sent to you automatically by setting this alert. Great tool for the tool box.

Internet has no borders and can provide leads to red flags, further in-depth investigations and provide social media based reporting. Dive into the deep web to find your answers.

In a family case, I was tasked to find my client's child. The mother maintained a very low profile on the Internet and would be tough to find. Utilizing the name of her family members, we found her profile under simply her first name and last initial. Her profile was extremely secure and allowed no access to photos, personal information or pictures of the new child. Further searches of the family members identified her sister who had less security features on her profile. We found pictures of her sister and my client's newborn son. We identified his date of birth, full name and many pictures of his photos. We were able to provide the client with photographs from the hospital when he was born, his full name and date of birth, as well as new photographs as the child was now two-years-old. Never say never. We found all the information he required, and it only took some Internet sleuthing to find it.

Years ago, I was assigned a domestic case involving a missing child. I got on a plane to Houston, rented a car, and drove to a small rural community in East Texas looking for a kidnapped child. That's Gumshoe – without the Internet or a

cell phone. Ah, those were the good old days.

The Interview and Interrogation

This element of the investigation is critical to your success. You need things that you don't learn through a formal education or are taught in your home. And many times, after you've left the interview room – you'll say to yourself, "Oh, I meant to ask this." It happens to the best of us.

Efficient interviewing is a specialized skill that must be learned by training and experience. We cannot teach you experience, we cannot give you common sense, but we can offer you some basic training concepts in the proper way to conduct various interviews.

An investigator/interviewer must develop an intuition of how to proceed on each case. Being prepared and well informed about your case and the client instructions will begin to lead you along the path to completing a successful assignment. And all that begins by being a great listener. People will volunteer a great deal more information than you imagine, if you listen with your ear first.

No investigator is empowered to force an interview. Only courts, people with color of authority, and legislative bodies etc., have this authority. There are two general methods that are applicable for influencing the state of mind of witnesses and suspects:

- One method involves physical or mental abuse. This is never allowed! <u>Under no circumstances can abuse or coercion be justified</u>.

- The other method involves conducting the interview in a humane and friendly atmosphere.

The qualities and personal attributes required to be a good interviewer can usually be developed with training and practice. Here are a few of the more important qualities of an interviewer:

- Honesty and Integrity - with the ability to impress upon all interviewees that you seek only the truth

- The ability to establish a rapport quickly and under many diverse conditions

- The ability to listen to the interviewee and evaluate responses

- The ability to maintain self-control during interviews and not become emotionally involved in the investigation

- Never pre-judge a witness.

- Find a common ground to make the surroundings more comfortable and the interviewee more at ease.

- Set aside all personal prejudices.

- Keep an open mind to all information.

- Don't share personal information to gain their confidence.

- Never exhibit sarcasm, anger or disgust. Be clear with information you're given.

- Don't talk down to the interviewee on any level – and that includes educational, mental or emotional levels.

- Never promise something you can't deliver.

- Maintain control of the interview.

- Be a great listener.

- Be extremely patient.

Statements:

A private investigator may be asked to simply interview a person, or take handwritten notes, record the conversation with the interviewee's permission, or take a statement under oath with a court reporter present. These statements include:

- Identify the witness by full name, date of birth, address, driver's license number, and in the U.S. their social security number.

- If the statement is handwritten, have the interviewee initial the bottom of each page, and sign the last page that "the above ... under penalty of perjury, the above .... Pages and .... Lines represent a true and accurate statement of the events and is true and correct to the best of my knowledge."

- If you sense they are hesitant or won't sign the last page, make a mistake somewhere in the statement. They'll discover your mistake. Then ask them to correct your mistake in their own handwriting, and initial it to show they have read the statement to that point.

- In handwritten statements, never use paragraphs. You don't want to give anyone an excuse to say that you added information after they signed the document.

- Give them a copy of the statement to make sure both of your records reflect the same information.

- According to the Ibrahim Rule in Canada, for a statement to be admissible, it must be taken under oath and clear of duress.

- It is illegal in Canada to record the conversation of two people without their permission. In the U.S. one cannot record a conversation legally unless they are a party to the conversation. The eaves-dropping and wire-tapping between two or more parties that excludes the investigator is left to the experts.

- Avoid disclosing any company, confidential, or privileged information to anyone, and that includes the interviewee.

- If they decline to sign the statement, ask them to sign their name that they decline to sign the statement. You'd be surprised how many people will.

How to Take Notes:

Preferably, notes should be clearly handwritten (in your own language) on only one side of a page. This is especially important when the loose-leaf type notebook is used, and the notes are removed for testifying. (NOTE: Do not destroy your written report, even if the final typewritten report has been completed unless it's your company or client's policy.) Notes must be clearly identified with numbered pages, the date and time, the location, complete address, name and phone number, when the notes were taken, the case number, and as clearly as possible, identify the parties with all their pertinent information. Use only common abbreviations that leave no room for interpretation. If you have more than one person and don't want to continue repeating their name throughout the report, give each of them a letter of the alphabet the first time you insert their name. And all subsequent individuals receive their own letter of the alphabet. Do the reports as quickly as possible after the information is developed. Today's PI uses a recorder or Dragon Speak.

Make sure your notes are complete with all the information gathered, are concise, and contains no personal opinions.

It's not necessary to write down every word. Primarily you need to also be listening. Don't interrupt. Make yourself a note and let them complete their thoughts. When it's your turn, bring your question in. It's called respect, and you'll learn more.

One investigator attended an accused serial killer's trial as required. The witness was answering a critical question that gave the attorney more

valuable information. But the attorney was focused

on his next question, interrupted the witness, missed

the great info, and rushed past the information.

Thankfully, an investigator was sitting behind the

attorney and passed a note to counsel.

Sketches

They are as important as photographs. No

one expects it to be to scale, and if you ask the

witness to draw it, be sure to identify everything: the

street, the location of north in relation to the

accident, the cars, the bed, the gun, whatever they

saw in their capacity as witness. And have them date,

time, and sign the sketch.

Principle Tools of Interviewing:

Many books have been written on the subject of body language. Internal attitudes are revealed in subtle ways: A nod, a shrug, or hand gestures. Is the witness leaning forward or back? Are their hands folded in their laps or are the arms crossed? Are the legs flat on the ground or crossed? Does the body face you or away? An emotional state may be revealed by a facial expression, a smile, a tear, laughter, inflection or tone of voice, etc.

Questions are the principle tools of interviewing. Never ask an open-ended question that the witness can respond to with a simple "yes" or a "no." An example of a bad question might be, "Do you work for living?" After a "yes" or a "no" response, you have to ask the next question. Don't waste time. To the point, ask, "What do you do for a

169

living?" Get that person talking and expanding on his/her response. Your phrasing is very important. Good question construction includes:

- Make questions short and confined to one topic.

- Seek answers to the "who, what, when, why, where, and how."

- Don't ask multiple-questions in one sentence.

- Questions should be clear, and easily understood.

- Avoid the use of frightening words like fraud, arson, murder. Use milder terms like mistake, missing money, the fire, accident, etc.

- Sometimes do what attorneys do all the time – ask questions that you already know the answers to.

- Don't assume you already know the right answer. The interviewee may know another reason his response is accurate – to him.

- Avoid leading questions in order to have the interviewee give you the response you want.

- Don't do the attorney-type questioning that contains double or triple negatives. They are confusing, and you'll often get a poor response. You hear those all the time by TV lawyers. "It isn't true, is it that…"

- Pose your questions from the general information to the specific. i.e. "Where did the accident occur?" Then, "How many lanes was Sunset Blvd in each direction?" "Which lane were you in?" "Does the street run north and south or east and west? "What day of the week was it?" "What time did it occur?"

"Describe the weather conditions for me."

- Encourage the interviewee in free narrative of the event. Remember to listen.

- At the conclusion of the interview, summarize what they've told you to make sure you have it accurate in your mind.

- Thank them for taking their time and for the generosity of the information, and leave the door open in the event more questions arise.

In the event of an indirect approach to the interview, in some cases it's necessary to conceal the true purpose of fact gathering. This form of interview is known as elicitation in Canada and called sub-rosa in the U.S. The investigator hides their true identify and the area of interest. It's often a brief approach, limited in scope, and used to develop more leads.

- Your undercover story should be simple and believable. "I went to high school with John, but I've lost touch with him. Do you have any idea where he is now? We're planning a high school reunion," is a simple example.

- Don't hold yourself out to be an expert on a subject you aren't completely familiar with.

- Pose your investigation to obtaining only the facts that you need to take you to the next step(s).

- Create simple props if you need them. (Specific clothing—but never police uniforms, forms, a clipboard, etc.)

- Most importantly, unless you are told otherwise, <u>always clear your approaches through your client and your employer</u>!

Impersonation Laws:

Generally, the indirect method cannot be used if it violates the statutes and laws of the state, federal, and/or province in either the U.S. or Canada. These include things like impersonating an officer or agent of any legally organized society or institution, misrepresenting oneself as a military member by using discharge buttons, campaign ribbons, etc. When the name of an organization or company has to be used, it must be a fictitious company. You never want to cause a real organization to be exposed to a lawsuit, cause them financial loss, injury, worry or embarrassment.

Did you know people sometimes don't want to get involved? Please keep in mind that potentially friendly and co-operative witnesses still may not give desired information for a number of reasons:

- They have faulty perception or simply don't remember.

- They do not completely understand what is wanted.

- They are not aware that they possess worthwhile information.

- They are reluctant to get involved or involve others.

- They are not impressed with the importance of co-operating.

- They're not friendly toward the investigator or the client.

- They have been threatened or are fearful.

- They dislike possible inconvenience of appearing in court.

- They are unknowingly prejudiced.

- Their logic or conclusions are faulty.

- They mistake inferences for facts.

- They are mentally incapacitated, nervous or have low intelligence.

Sometimes, when they do cooperate, you'll spot some clues that they know more than they're telling you. Look for these:

- They attempt to evade the question.

- They offer vague responses.

- Look at their body language.

- Let them know that you were specifically told that they know more.

- Sometimes they know more because they were at the scene or somehow involved.

- Their response contains inconsistencies from what you already know.

- You may need to rephrase the question later in the interview to clarify an earlier question.

Test Assertions:

Even when people believe they're telling you the truth, you should always test their assertions. It's critical to separate the falsehoods from the facts. Drill down on the most minute of questions to make sure there's no mistaking the truth. One word that usually will trigger this instinct in you is the interviewee using the words, "I think..." Why do they think that? That's your job. Inferences are different than gossip or guessing. Separate the fact from the fiction.

Second, evaluate the reliability of the witness. Are they personally involved, mentally competent, or simply need attention? Remember, a lot of arsonists, for example, stay at the scene to become a witness and stay close to the investigating departments. A number of murderers attend the funeral of their victims and often visit the gravesite after everyone has gone or on special dates that only mean something to the murderer and the victim like the victim's birthday, or anniversary of death.

One of the most difficult witnesses to catch is the chronic liar. They've done it all their lives, and no one has ever called them on it. Sometimes, they're simply motivated to impress others and build a sense of self-importance and self-worth. He/she will frequently be recognized by his or her tendency to brag, exaggerate accomplishments and abilities, and continually make assertions about the difficulties he or she has experienced in their lives.

Drawing inferences and conclusions from the interview:

The results of an interview are measured by accomplishing/completing the principle investigative objectives. First of all, the information obtained must be relevant and material. If the testimony is to be used in court, the facts must be admissible under the rules of evidence.

Most of the difficulty of drawing conclusions and evaluating evidence too early comes from a failure to get all available facts together before making a decision and testing them. Do not draw conclusions until you have completed the interview and use care when you do interpret them.

An interviewer should know and appreciate that physical influence factors enter into play when analyzing the truth, accuracy, and completeness of the information they are given. Some of these factors are:

- Smoking decreases both mental and physical efficiencies.

- The emotional factor involved as it's revealed by the smoking frequency during the interview.

- Opiates, including opium morphine, and heroin, plus pain killing medications have a depressant effect on the body.

- Cocaine is a stimulant that rushes the intellect for a short period of time followed by a deep feeling of depression.

- Alcohol that produces changes in the brain and nervous system by removing normal inhibitions.

With the factors listed above in the interviewee's system, you need to recognize them by their symptoms. He or she needs to be sufficiently sober to be aware of his or her constitutional rights and in full possession of his or her faculties. Thus, it's always best to reschedule the interview until a time when the person's body is clean and clear of those stimulants.

A few keys factors that may help you identify the factors are listed below, to aid you in knowing if you should continue with the interview or reschedule.

- A feeling of well-being
- Exultation (lively or joy)
- Increased self-confidence
- Loss of judgment
- Loquaciousness (talkative)

- Dulling of the senses

- Loss of skill

- Slurred speech

- Disturbance of equilibrium

- Visual disturbance of color, motion, and
  distance perception

- Apathy (lack of emotion)

- Tremors

- Cessation of automatic movements

- Sweating

- Dilation of surface capillaries

- Stupor

Intoxicated individuals have a reduced ability to fabricate lies. However, they also have an impairment of the sense organs and a reduction in judgment and reasoning power. For this reason, be cautious of evidence observed by an intoxicated person, as well as evidence reported by a witness while he is under the influence of alcohol.

Other variables add to a less-than-excellent interview. Consider stimulants like those found in both coffee and tea. The efficiency of the physical and mental processes may be increased by as much as 4% by consumption of moderate amounts of caffeine. During extended interviews, the use of these beverages might increase the source's mental alertness and assist them in the process or remembering details.

Interviewing children:

Hunger and thirst also distracts from a good interview, as does the age of the person. Children often make good witnesses because they lack the maturity to filter out information that an adult would not observe. Having said that, a vivid imagination may also distort information. Some children are exceptionally susceptible to suggestions, and they will answer what they believe you want to hear, rather than respond in truth.

- Determine who might have influenced the child's response by giving or "feeding" them with information.

- Make sure the questions contain clear age-appropriate words.

- Work at their level with expressions and words they know.

- Check with adults: parents, treating physicians, and teachers to determine their reliability.

- Test the children with questions asking them a word, and then asking them to tell you what it means. The one most often tested in court is, "What does telling the truth mean to you?"

- Make the interview short and clear. Children don't have a long attention span, and they tire easily.

Qualifying a witness:

Some people are experts in the fields that affect your case. It might be their employment history, education, or hobbies. Whether it's a CPA, a scientist, a mechanic or a plumber, people have information that will educate you on your case, and often times refer to someone else who may know more than they do.

You'll always find someone in the neighborhood who loves or despises the person you're inquiring about. Find them both. Each brings information that will help and hurt the case against that person. It also leads you to others who may know even more.

How to Recognize Psychological Factors

A number of psychological (emotional) factors come into play when you're fact-gathering:

- Anger

- Fear

- Neutral involvement

- Relationship to the case

Those emotions affect how the individual will respond and react to the investigation, and should be measured and evaluated accordingly.

With anger, physical attacks may be boiling below the surface. The individual might be angry for any number of reasons including being interrupted from their duties, anger against your client, the person or company involved, the cause, any number of reasons. Be aware of and try your best to neutralize them in advance.

If the individual is fearful, they are concerned with either any clear and present or imagined danger. They know something unpleasant that affects their job, their future, their lives, or the lives of someone they know. Help them by resolving the non-existent issues and offering to find a better solution.

Neutrality affects the interviewer who anticipates the witness might have a wrong perception of the purpose of the interview and be fearful and/or anger. Neutralize it with reassurances. That's your job.

Conditioned responses exhibit themselves through emotions that can result in exaggeration, denying, or down-right lying. You'll observe them through:

- Dryness of mouth

- Restlessness - frequent change in position; tapping of feet; fidgeting; gripping arms of chairs; elbows held tight to the body

- Fanning hands through the air; chewing fingernails; pencils or other objects; biting lips or inside cheeks

- Excessive sweating - particularly of the hands or in armpits

- Carotid artery pulsation

- Unusual changes in complexion - pallid or ruddy complexion

- Excessive nervous swallowing

- Avoiding looking directing at the interviewer

- Statements of truthfulness in excessive numbers, like, "I hope to die if I'm lying," or "I swear on my dead mother's grave."

- Vague responses using words like, "I'm not sure," "I don't remember," "I don't think."

Perception:

Perception is the process of receiving knowledge through the sense organs - sight, hearing, smell, taste, and touch. Any defects from the norm can result in faulty testimony especially in the areas of sight (glass prescriptions) and hearing (aids). Age, medical, and emotional conditions may also impair their impressions. For example, 3% of the world's population are color blind.

Memory:

The time lapse between the event and the interview also affects the memory. If it's a long time, try word-association to some event. "Where were you on 9/11?" Or relate the event to something the individual can relate to. Talk to a witness as soon as possible.

Be very suspicious of witnesses or sources who recall and recount complete details of an occurrence but cannot remember other more important aspects of the incident. Or if you hear the very same data from several sources. They've been talking with each and have their stories down pat. Why do you think police put multiple suspects and independent witnesses in separate cars, then once at the police station in separate rooms?

Bias

Who hasn't met someone who may be biased or prejudiced and gives distorted information, either intentionally or unintentionally? It could be something as simple as a witness's belief that alcohol is bad. Therefore, his/her belief might conclude the neighbor who drinks is a drunk. Information can be colored both in a positive or a negative light based on the witness's bias.

Deception:

From time to time and situation to situation, persons of all ages and cultures use some form of deception to compensate for personal inadequacies. In most cases, such conduct is resorted to when the individual feels incapable or is unprepared to solve a problem by more desirable means. Sometimes, it's their attempt to escape from the consequences of their deeds, puff up the value of their allegations or testimony or reveal something negative about themselves.

Jury Consulting Services

High-profile and high-stake criminal and civil jury trials create a need for professional jury consulting companies that provide experts with special skills for honing in on the right jury to best represent the attorney's client's best end result – innocent or a favorable financial verdict. These employees are human behavior experts whose sole responsibility is to help the attorneys gain a winning edge.

Often times, they're highly educated in the fields of behavioral science, sociology, political science, criminology, psychology, or other social science. These consultants are hired for their common sense, intuitiveness, and knowledge of the human behavior.

They conduct research, create pretrial profiles, and generally assist the attorneys to develop trial strategies that lead to a winning outcome.

Because of their education, background, and success in their field, they generally are highly paid for their services. Do these people succeed? High profile cases such as O.J. Simpson, Oprah, Martha Stewart, and Casey Anthony prove their value. Ask Dr. Phil.

Locates

Private investigators are often tasked to locate individuals for many purposes. Knowing the reason that the client wants the person located is imperative, as it will provide insight as to the reason the subject may be hiding or not. It will set the stage for the rest of your investigation.

If the person is being located because they witnessed an accident or incident, the individual may be easier to find than a person that is hiding from a debt collection agency. There are various reasons a person may be hiding and not want to be found. This could not even be related to your case, so it is important to know the reasons.

In Canada, such locates must be clearly documented in your file to remain within the privacy law and regulations. Since Private Investigators are not debt collectors, and only hired to find the person and provide details to clients, the task may not warranted unless there is a lot of money owing. In other situations, we need to be careful because the client could have other reasons for seeking the information. An abusive spouse or a stalker, both with personal reasons, could cause serious harm to the subject of the investigation. For these reasons, investigator must choose their cases wisely at all times to protect the public.

Information Client provides:

- Subject's name
- Last known address
- Last known telephone number(s)
- Date of Birth
- Spouse
- Family make up

- Previous address, telephone number

- Reason for Investigation

When tasked to conduct locates, insure that the client provides all details that is in their file related to the subject. This will enable you to complete the task to the best of your ability. Insure that your file is well-documented, if the matter is a locate for the purpose of service of documents, ask the client to provide the court file number so that you have back-up.

Public Documentation

In Canada with strict privacy laws, there is no central database to search a person across the country and provide a full detailed report. The access to information is extremely limited and searches have to be completed by Province or Region, often in person. Some Provinces do have a central database for court searches and corporation reports. To identify the available online information, search the Province to determine the public documentations available. Searches such as land ownership, corporation profiles, lien registration, and bankruptcy and court documents may provide clues and insight when tracking a person down. Also there is Federal Privacy Legislation and some Provincial Privacy Legislation, so it is important to know the laws where the investigation is being conducted.

In the United States, there are a number of resources for full database searches that provide a comprehensive report on the individual. Some searches are only accessible to registered organizations with PI firms and agencies able to register for the data, as they utilize it to identify

crime, fraud, court orders and illegal activities with

strict privacy regulations for those who are able to

order the reports. These reports provide more details

on an individual such as related address, people, and

pertinent information that would assist you in

locating the subject.

After determining laws around the access to

information, then you will have the proper tools to

locate an individual. This can be completed in other

ways, such as neighborhood inquiries and previous

employers, Internet profile searches and any leads

that were identified through public documentation.

Good luck and dig deeper if they are evading service. Of course, you can always utilize surveillance and wait for them to leave and serve them on the way out the door. Can you outrun that dog?

Loss Prevention

Some investigators are hired full time or part time to conduct loss prevention services for companies. Sometimes they will be hired for a store with a high shoplifting loss record and watch for potential shoplifters or fake slip and falls. They also identify high risk areas where in-store cameras or more visibility by store employees should be focused, thus reducing risks of injury or loss. They're also helpful in other areas:

- Hired to design a plan to prevent theft
- Identify high risk areas for injury or loss
- Identify employees with potential criminal activity
- Conduct routine inspections for managers, store representatives, or the Home Office

- Price checking of items, including sales items

- Accident scene photographs and secure the area

- Interviews and statements

These positions can be highly desirable, especially when you're assigned to a chain of grocery or department stores that suffer enormous financial losses annually. This is job security– for you and your company.

Marine Investigations

Much like automobile or aircraft insurance policies, the investigator may be assigned to a case for a number of reasons. Primarily, they should have a Small Boat Piloting License, or a Piloting License, and a very extensive knowledge of nautical terms and how boats operate in general. Whether someone is hurt on the boat, there's been a boating accident (some during sanctioned or unsanctioned races or just pleasure sailing), the boat's allegedly missing by either theft or sinking, whatever the case, that investigator must have marine experience. In the U.S. if the incident occurred in some areas, they're protected under several federal laws that the investigator must be familiar with.

For injuries to sailors, longshoremen, and dock workers, the Jones Act, also known as the

Merchant Marine Act of 1920, Section 27, identifies the responsibility to the injured party:

"Any sailor who shall suffer personal injury in the course of his employment may, at his election, maintain an action for damages at law, with the right to trial by jury, and in such action all statutes of the United States modifying or extending the common-law right or remedy in cases of personal injury to railway employees shall apply..."

This federal law allows sailors to bring actions against ship owners based on claims of un-seaworthiness or negligence whether the injury or damage is intentional or not.

The Longshore and Harbor Workers' Compensation Act, commonly referred to as the "Longshore Act" or "LHWCA" also created in 1927, covers certain maritime workers, including most dock workers and maritime workers not otherwise covered by the Jones Act. In addition, Congress extended the LHWCA to cover some U.S. workers on the outer continental shelf, and those working for U.S. government contractors on foreign soil and/or on the water.

Basic investigation includes techniques like those in other cases as stated earlier in this manual: Statements, photographs, copies of all documents relating to ownership of the vessel, copies of all medical and professional reports, an understanding of the terms, conditions, and exclusions contained in the insurance policy, witness reports, reports from the Coast Guard or other policing authority that protects that body of water where the incident occurred,

Fraud is rampant in boat losses. When times are good, people buy boats. When they can't sell them during bad times; people sink or burn them or sell them to someone out of the country. This also happens with new high end cars that have a huge loan balance.

On one case, the Insured told his carrier that someone had stolen his boat. The investigator went to the residence and did not find a trailer. She inquired of neighbors, and they were surprised to learn that the Insured ever owned a boat. She asked the Insured for evidence of purchase (canceled check, loan docs, state registration papers, etc.) He had none. He told the investigator that this was a boat the Insured had dreamed of owning. It was his pride and joy. He told her they had just taken the boat to a nearby lake for the weekend with friends and had a great time. She asked for photos of the fun time – he denied having any. He did, however, file a boat theft report with the local police department.

She contacted every boat dealer in the area where the Insured lived and discovered that one dealer had some boat registration papers stolen his office. They're like a doctor's prescription form and contain numbers (like car license plate numbers).

She contacted the Insured's agent and asked to see a boat photograph that would have been and should have been placed in the insurance company's underwriting file as proof a boat existed. He had taken a "phone order" that included only a description of the vessel and a "registration number" less than thirty days earlier that happened to be one of the stolen numbers.

The insured was arrested for filing a false report and spent considerable time in a county jail.

Does it surprise you to know there was no boat – ever?

On another case, the insurance company paid $175,000 for a large boat that the Insured claimed a whale sunk off the Catalina coast of California. And once they paid the claim, thought someone should take another look.

The Insured was an Assistant District Attorney (ADA) in a nearby state. The investigator flew to that state and interviewed the Insured. Convinced that the Insured was lying, she told him her next trip to his office would be with the FBI.

After several years of investigation up and down the California coast, she found the boat in Mexico. She and another investigator that spoke

Spanish, were driven to the border, met with an attorney, hired two men as pilots, and they commandeered the boat and brought it back to Terminal Island where the FBI met them.

What joy to travel to the ADA's office with the agents and return him to California where a court gave him twenty years in a federal pen?

Imagine the shock on his face to meet the investigator again. Gotta love it.

Online Database Resources vs. Library

Online databases provide an advantage in time in comparison to the library. When searching the available online databases, we don't have to leave our offices. Although again the information is only as accurate as the clerk entering the data.

There are a number of online resources that help us get information at rapid speed listed below. Please note that this list is just a start!

- Online residential databases - .411.ca

- Google maps, street view and images

- Obituaries Announcements

- Government sites that show corporation documents

- Website, Domain and IP address Searches – Whois Look up

Library

When conducting cold cases, lost family members, and adoption investigations, often there is a need to seek outdated information from other resources. This is where the library has kept endless records from the past and are available to the public. It is a great resource when you are assigned a file where the information is old.

Some libraries also offer a per cost search to find the information that you are requesting and although this is beneficial if the cost is reasonable, it is important when these searches are completed fully, as it will be used in a report, it is better that the investigator attend in person to insure that all information has been found and reported.

Resources in reference libraries

- Dated City Directories and telephone books

- Ancestry, voting list and tax documents

- Old newspapers – wedding and death announcements

- School yearbooks

In cold case and old investigations, we must work from the last known date that could be over fifty-years-old, and work forward to find the information. There is a wealth of information at the library, as the old city directories contained more detailed information including spouses, children and employment. A library reference clerk is always available to walk you through the microfiche and old documents.

In a child custody case, we knew that the mother of the client's son had been charged with dangerous driving causing death. In Canada, we were unable to access any of the criminal documents, as per our privacy laws, and no

information was online about the accident. We went

to the public library and researched the three-year

period when she was driving without a driver's

license from a bar in town, and lost control hitting a

pole, and her passenger was instantly killed. By

following through the newspaper articles, we were

able to establish the date of the accident followed by

the dates of trial, and the continued newspaper

coverage. We printed the documents and was able to

include them as evidence in our court brief for the

judge.

Patent Infringement

These investigations are conducted much like everything that's covered in this manual: interviews, note-taking, statements, documenting evidence, photos, reports, surveillance, civil and criminal searches, everything...but the investigation goes further.

What is patent infringement? One party manufacturers, imports, uses, sells, or offers for sale some technology or product. In America, they register it with the U.S. Patent Office that covers a specific term limit. If the technology or product is used by someone in another country where there's no patent pending, it's considered to be infringed upon.

Every country has its own test on whether the technology or product is exactly like the one, almost like the one, or similar to the one being questioned. The investigator reads the claim of the technology or product involved in the patent. Even if one element doesn't match or is missing, it's often said that the other claimant does not infringe the patent.

The investigator needs to review the allegations and determine:

- Was it practicing the patented invention?
- Has the patent expired?
- Was it performing in any infringing matter in the territory covered by the patent?
- Does it contain a defect that makes the patent invalid or unenforceable?
- Has a new license been obtained?

One investigation involved an assignment on a popular water-proofing material uses for exterior wood surfaces. Simply enough, a patent was in place in every country on earth, and one clear photo of the

product against the infringer revealed an obvious

infringement. The color and size of the container, the

almost identical wording (including the marketing

material), and the ingredients were identical. And

the most obvious – the name of the product had been

altered by only one letter.

Sometimes, the investigation is just that easy.

Professional Security Risks Audit

The investigator is often engaged to conduct professional security audits. These are important to the safety of clients, customers, complying with city, state, federal, or national laws, and can often be identified and corrected immediately. They may include:

- Identifying high risk areas
- Providing a plan to secure these areas and fill in the holes
- Note potential areas as high and low risk
- Recommend solutions to security needs

One case involved a larger than number of alleged "slip and falls" at a large California grocery chain. By reviewing the scene, it was clear that no camera was focused in that area, and the aisle was partially hidden from the meat market or anywhere near the front where an employee might

observe a potential fake injury. Also, the store had a

second floor area where the supervisors conducted

their paperwork. The investigator also recommended

that windows be cut through the solid wall that

afforded a complete picture of action on the floor,

and monitors were installed on everyone's desk

upstairs. The fake claims dropped 98%, thus

increasing their bottom-line profit and reducing

their insurance premiums.

Reports

Reports are the written account of something that a private investigator has observed, heard, or found. It is even more than that for an investigator as it reflects the work completed with lack of any opinion or bias. As Matlock used to say, "Just the facts."

Agencies and firms have a policy for investigators with the outline of the report format that is used and preferred by them. It is important to know the work flow on reports to be submitted for work completed. A surveillance investigator may be very different from a background investigation report. However, your employer will dictate the format and requirements.

In surveillance reports, the necessary information should be in every report.

- File name and number

- Date
- Weather conditions at the time of surveillance
- Equipment used – Type of Video Camera, Still Camera, Recorder, etc.
- Description of the property that you surveilling
- Vehicles and license plates parked on the driveway
- Description of subject when first observed, including physical and clothing
- Time and observation of activity
- Time terminated
- Time finished report

Background Investigation reports should include the file name, number, and date and time that the research or inquiries were conducted. It is important to note that this type of report will flow differently than a surveillance report, as you may have to wait for search results or more leads on the file. This type of report will again be outlined by the investigative company in their policy.

It is important to note that all reports should be completed at the soonest available time to insure accuracy and void of opinion.

Reputational Due Diligence Investigations

These types of investigation are to establish the reputation of an individual or company to determine the suitability and reputation of potential business partners. Due Diligence investigation provides the client with insight about the reputation of a company in the respected industry. It identifies the corporation profile, along with the directors and shareholders of the subject business. There are a number of areas that identify that provide insight for potential partners or investors. This will provide the client with an informative report about the company that they will use to base their decision on. The following may be part of the reputational due diligence process.

- Registered Corporation Report

- Registered Tax Number and last date filed taxes

- Site Visit

- Shareholders information

- Stock market information

- Reputational inquiries with trade groups, competitors, newspapers, government, etc.

- Media search on the principals, and the corporation

- Negative media search for corruption and bribery

- A comprehensive report providing all the information found

Reputational due diligence investigations are delicate, and discretion is extremely important to a successful outcome. The client does not want the subject corporation to determine that they evaluating the risk of investing or forming a partnership as it could sour the relationship if it came to light.

On the other hand, an investor or partner must be aware of any issues prior to entering into such a contract. Better safe than sorry later!

Social Media

Although we have covered much off this in earlier chapters, the explosion of this resource only enhances our ability to obtain information that can lead us to reliable information. Therefore, this chapter is totally dedicated to social media profiles that can provide leads to other investigative roads. Clearly you must know the purpose of your investigation and what you are looking for, otherwise the social media accounts can be overwhelming.

In particular, when researching on Facebook, LinkedIn, Twitter and Instagram, as these are the most popular at this time, note the people that are following your subject. Comb all the publically available information. If you find another person who consistently likes or comments on the social media account, take a good look at the third party profile, their friends and pictures, as they may provide leads to other roads to find the information on your subject.

On LinkedIn, you can look at those who have recommended the professional, to see how they are connected.

It is important to note the following when conducting social media searches. On Facebook, if you check a person's profile regularly, when they go to their home page it may ask them if you want to be their friend, so be cautious. Get everything you can the first time. Print it to insure that your evidence remains intact and usable.

On LinkedIn, if you are signed into your account, then the person who you check can see that you visited their profile. This is a free service for the last five people that have viewed your site. You would need to set your account to anonymous or simply sign out and review the information. It may not give you the full profile, however the information may be sufficient for the purpose of your investigation. It is important to keep updated on the changes in all social media if you are utilizing it.

We do not recommend investigators developing fake profiles and adding subjects as a friend, as the law is still testing this with some case law but not enough to insure you will not be the test case. Social media information is still scrutinized by your client and the courts.

We were hired to complete an Internet social media search on a female. She alleged while sitting on a bus a boy had touched her inappropriately.

What was her reputation? Both individuals were

under the age of sixteen and active online. Her

profile was very secure. Through searches, we found

her best friend whose privacy settings were

unrestricted. In her photographs, we found a ton of

pictures of the complainant and even ones that

showed her in very sexy outfits, plus exposing her

breasts. This was only part of the investigation, as

we did background, it was determined that the

accused was not even on the bus on the date she said

the incident happened. If you post it or your friend

posts it, I am going to find it....that is my motto.

Specialty Searches

When given an assignment that requires work outside of the investigator's territory or expertise, find the right partner to complete the work. You'll generally find them in your local, state, federal, or international organizations:

- Provide detailed instructions of the information requested.

- Obtain a quote for the work.

- Verify the credentials and qualifications of the investigator.

- Confirm they are an expert in their field.

- Specialty searches may include engineer, accident reconstruction, forensic accountant, arson investigator, etc.

Staged Accidents

Investigators are often hired when there appears to be some inconsistencies in a motor vehicle accident. Often, this occurs when the damage on the vehicles involved do not match. Sometimes the same four passengers in each vehicle claim not to know each other, and the passengers don't go to the police station or the police aren't called to the scene. This is an organized effort by groups of people that scheme and plan the accident for financial gain. There are a number of groups involved, including the driver of each vehicle, the tow truck driver, the auto body shop, the paralegal, the clinic. Yes, and the passengers that are "parachuted" or buy seats in the car. This type of fraud investigation is more intense and requires in-depth reports. As there are so many aspects to this type of case, it is important to report on each person involved separately with no reference of others in the group. A court brief can be built on each person for the Insurer, their counsel, and the police.

Review for investigation

- Engineers report – re-accident details

- Accident report

- Witness statements

- Claim forms submitted to the Insurer

- Auto body, paralegal, clinic or rehab and other service providers information

Once all this information has been received and a full review is completed, then the real work begins. A database may be utilized to assist in determining if any of the individuals involved are related in other ways, such as name, address, and telephone numbers. There may also be employers listed that could be entered into the database. Once this has been completed you can run a number of charts to see if any information relates to more than one person in the car. After the cross reference has been completed, a scene visit may for obstructions, video cameras and other potential witnesses maybe completed.

Inquiries to conduct:

- Corporation profile on paralegal, clinic, auto body shop and tow company

- Inspection at clinic, auto body shop

- Site visit – paralegal

- Witnesses

- Video evidence secured

- Service providers interviewed

- Employers interviewed

- Full report on each individual involved in the accident and follow up on any leads that have been identified.

It is difficult to know where the investigation will take you. However, it is important to follow all leads. If this group is involved in this type of activity, more than likely there are plenty other accidents where all parties are involved, and the evidence needs to be documented so that it can be provided to the lawyers and insurers, to decide whether they are seeking a criminal or civil remedy.

In one case that I worked on, there was a blanket policy for a car repair shop. There were 19 different accidents with at least four passengers in each car, with a total of 55 claimants and an estimated loss of $5 million. We identified the warning telephone number used by three different *passenger in three different collisions. Clinic*

inspections were completed, service providers were

interviewed, and court briefs were presented to the

police on each individual involved. In the end, the

police re-interviewed all the passengers and drivers,

and eventually determined that many were not even

in the car at the time of the accident. There were

only two legitimate claims, and the rest were

withdrawn. Some criminal charges were laid, and

the insurer was extremely happy with the outcome.

Surveillance

Surveillance can be defined as the secretive and continuous observation of persons, places, and things necessary to document information of their activities. It is a technique that establishes solid proof of the facts that may be in question. Is my husband cheating on me? Is that man really crippled?

It's often tiring and boring work with one or two minutes of excitement when you get the subject in sight of your lens.

You will use some commonly-used terms when reporting your work to your client:

- Subject/Claimant is the person being observed.

- The "surveillant" is you, the investigator.

- "Burned" is a term used to indicate that the investigator has been discovered by the subject.

- "Covert" means the surveillance is secret or hidden from the subject.

- "Open covert" is rare and is performed when the client doesn't care if the subject knows what's going on.

- "Tail" means to follow the subject.

- "Eyeball" can mean that the subject sees the investigator, and it can also mean that the investigator can eyeball the subject, but cannot be seen.

- "Loose" is a form of viewing the subject from a discreet distance.

- "Tight" is the opposite of loose. The investigator follows the subject very closely, but makes sure they aren't burned.

Patience is a huge asset. Success takes a long time and surveillance can be very tiring. You'll need to **adjust or adapt** to rapidly changing situations whether it's the subject's actions or a change in the weather. This ability could mean the difference in being recognized (burned) by the subject, or overlooked and accepted by him as being someone of no particular concern. **Resourcefulness** is important because the investigator must have the ingenuity and intelligence to make adjustments when situations change. A passport for the airport, change for the toll road, bus, or subway, a credit card, wearing very comfortable shoes, and having extra batteries for the camera or an extra camera are just a few ideas here.

Be **alert.** You never know when some small detail is significant, i.e. dropping something in a mail box, making a phone call, handing off something to a stranger without speaking or shaking hands.

We've already covered the importance of field notes in this manual. The key to a successful investigation is having excellent notes that evolve into excellent reports. If you don't have time to write – dictate. Small digital USB products with twenty-seven hours of recording come in handy, especially at night when there's no light or when you're tailing the subject.

As with any investigation you conduct, if you have some acting experience and the ability to blend into the crowd, you'll be well on the way to becoming a great surveillant. Avoid looking eye-to-eye with the subject as they're more likely to remember you later. If you're asking directions, point up and down the street in distress, not eye-to-eye. Act natural and appear ordinary. Fit into the community and the crowd. Don't wear a nice three-piece suit in Haight Ashbury in San Francisco or Regent Park in Toronto. You're better off with worn jeans, a ragged flannel shirt, and sandals. A nice fake tattoo would be a good addition as would a nose or lip ring.

Don't wear items that the subject might think of later because you stood out. So eliminate T-shirts with cute sayings, college or sports logos. In other words, don't draw unnecessary attention to yourself in their memory. And stay away from uniforms of firemen or anyone with the color of authority. In some states and countries – it's considered illegal to impersonate a policing authority.

Know your case, look for the truth, and be prepared to improvise.

An investigator received a worker's compensation assignment to observe a subject over a long holiday weekend. The subject had always shown up at hearings in a wheelchair and claimed great pain. Although a team of expert physicians could find nothing wrong with him, he continued to deny his ability to walk.

The investigator was shocked to see the subject the first day wearing a hockey uniform and walking to his car. She filmed him all the way to the field, and then drove to a quiet street and installed a magnetic sign on the side of her van using the name of a fake television station, and returned to the field to find the subject was the goalie!

She asked to interview the team and take film of the game that would be on the nightly news. Everyone agreed and even proudly signed photo-releases. The subject jumped high, kicked proudly, and reached in every direction defending his goal trying to impress the investigator as much as he could for film time. Boy did he!

That next hearing, the subject appeared as usual with a caregiver pushing his wheelchair and moaning in pain. The investigator walked in and rolled the film for the hearing officer. The subject had been on worker's comp benefits for many months. The hearing officer ordered the subject to repay all the monies paid, and the court confiscated his passport.

An interesting end to this story is that the subject called the insurance company a few months later after his family repaid them and requested a copy of the film. He was returning to his native country and wanted to show his family how he spent his time in America.

In some cases you may need to have an interpreter. Fortunately for the investigator mentioned above, the hockey coach spoke enough broken English to communicate with his team. The back of your van or trunk of your car should be filled with various tools to help you. Think of needing an umbrella in Seattle, a hat in Florida, or snow shoes in Canada.

Foot Surveillance can be conducted with one person, two people, or more.

The successful one-man foot surveillance requires the investigator position him/herself walking behind and to the left of the subject to ensure he/she doesn't get burned, but close enough to clearly document the activity.

When we look behind us, we tend to turn to the right and look directly behind us, so you'll always have time to stop and look casually at a store window, check your watch, or open the newspaper or magazine you might be holding to cover your camera.

With two investigators, change positions often, even from one side of the street to the other should be subject cross the street unexpectedly.

With three investigators, one of the three might be the driver that picks up one who can change clothes and disguises in the vehicle only to be dropped off at another location farther ahead of the subject. That third person might also be a substitute replacement if another investigator believes that he's been burned.

The surveillant should be alert to the methods subjects use to detect and elude surveillance, but don't misinterpret all of the subject's actions to think that the surveillance has been compromised. Some of these might include:

- Stopping abruptly and looking to the rear
- Casually looking around
- Suddenly revising his course
- Stopping abruptly after turning a corner
- Watching reflections in shop windows
- Entering a building and leaving immediately by another exit

- Walking slowly and then rapidly at alternate intervals

- Dropping something so the person can look around

- Stopping to tie shoelaces while looking around

- Using an associate or friend in a business to watch for surveillance

- Boarding a bus and riding a short distance or exiting just before it starts

- Circling the block in a taxi or private car

- In public places watching for persons peeking over or around newspapers

Once the subject has detected surveillance, he may use any of the following methods to elude the surveillance:

- Exits a bus or subway just as the doors are about to close

- Leaves a building through a rear or side exit or through a kitchen

- Loses himself in a crowd

- Uses a decoy

- Disappears down an alley. You do know not to follow him there, don't you?

- Changes appearance by using a form of disguise by changing clothes, hair style, wearing glasses, affecting a limp, etc.

If the subject enters an elevator, don't follow him unless there are several passengers to afford cover. Once inside, observe what floor he uses and select the floor above or below. Climbing up or down stairs will be your only choice here to catch up with the subject. And you run the risk of using the stairs and being confronted with fire safety doors that won't open from the stairway into the hall, only from the hallway OUT…be smart here.

If the subject is alone, hopefully, there'll be some elevator equipment on the wall to show what floor he exits. It's that simple.

If the subject enters a taxi, obtain the name and number of the cab and determine its destination for the subject. On a bus, sit behind the subject in case they exit quickly and without warning. Make it look like, "Gosh, I almost missed my stop, too."

If you're following the subject in a vehicle, follow all traffic signs, especially if they run a red light; make a dangerous U turn or left turn against the light. If you cannot legally follow them, try to pick up the tail at the earliest opportunity. If you lose them – start over from the beginning.

Public places like theaters, shopping centers, race tracks, concerts, etc. are the most difficult ones to follow the subject in. Here's their opportunity to casually drop or exchange something that will be picked up by an accomplice critical to your investigation.

In a restaurant or bar, stay close, but not obvious, and don't order a full meal, because they're as likely to jump up and exit as not. Start with a glass of water and languish over the menu until you determine his reasoning. If someone joins him, try to photograph him as discreetly as possible and attempt to identify him later.

If you lose your subject during surveillance, don't despair, it happens to us all. Accept that as perfectly normal, and attempt to relocate the subject and resume the investigation.

On criminal cases, it's not unusual for the subject to engage decoys or set traps to avoid surveillance. Think of "The Thomas Crown Affair" and hundreds of men in three-piece suits in a museum wearing bowler hats and carrying identical briefcases.

Sometimes it's very beneficial to engage a female investigator rather than a male. Females tend to be discounted by criminals especially because their wives don't work outside the home as a general rule. Also, females can get access to information with emotional touches that men don't have. And women tell women things they wouldn't share with men.

A number of male investigators tried on several occasions and using several approaches to catch a female CPA in criminal activity against her employer. That case involved hundreds of thousands of dollars over a ten-year period. The DA's office called in a female who scheduled an appointment in the lady's home. The host served tea and cookies while the female investigator discussed children in order to establish rapport. She had seen a number of photos of the subject's daughter in the living room. She talked about how hard it was to raise a daughter alone and how expensive children were as they grew.

As the casual conversation continued, the investigator noticed a visible physical change over the years in the daughter's photos and inquired about her health. The subject broke down and admitted that the daughter had been in and out of rehab, hooked on meth, lost her child to Children

Protective Services, and had almost been homeless,

until the co-dependent subject figured out a way to

pay the daughter's way to safety. Alas, it hadn't

worked. When the investigator asked how she had

funded her daughter's indiscretions, the subject

admitted that she regretted what she had to do to get

the money.

The investigator slammed her hand on the

coffee table startling the subject and said, "Honey,

why don't you just give me that second set of books,

okay?"

Once back at the office, the men laughed at

her and said, "Nothing, huh? We told you. There's

nothing there."

The investigator replied, "Boys, could you

help unload that second set of books from the trunk

of my car?" as she entered her office to complete her report.

As a post-script to that story – the female worked for thirty-seven years as a PI before retiring and having used her weapon only two times for her own safety.

Undercover

Undercover (also known as covert) operations may have many objectives that include obtaining evidence of a past, current, or future crime. Your assignment may be making sure people aren't violating the Criminal Codes of Canada and/or the United States, the *Occupational Health and Safety Act* (OSHA), the *Narcotics Control Act*, the *Liquor Control Act*, with illegal uses of alcohol or manufacture, use and/or sales of illegal drugs. The assignment may be to identify everyone engaged in those activities, determine how their operation is conducted, and recover the goods.

Often this type of work is performed by city, state, and/or federal policing authorities. However, it's possible that an investigator may be called in by a private client to conduct part of such work.

All reports will include observations, activities, photos, evidence, and statements (when required) exactly like those covered in other parts of this manual.

Any assignment requested that involves union activities, employee organizational activities, or collective bargaining activities should be declined and scrutinized. Employees have rights that an employer may simply not be able to get involved in by law.

Workplace Investigations

Workplace investigations are mainly mandatory in cases where there is alleged harassment, theft, workplace violence, fraud and any other type of dishonesty. In some cases, an employer may have their own staff that complete workplace investigations when an incident is reported or occurs. Employers may also have private agencies that investigate these types of allegations. This ensures that the investigation is impartial, external from the company, and does not violate any conflict of interest. The client or employer will usually instruct you as to their workplace safety policies.

In these types of investigations it is essential that the investigation be started within the first 48 hours to make sure that the person making the complaint has been addressed and has knowledge of the investigation. There are a few reason for this, if it is a workplace injury, then it is important to photograph the scene, obtain all video footage prior to its expiration and evidence could be tainted or lost.

In more serious cases, it is important to minimize the exposure to the company and employees.

The following steps can be taken to conduct the investigation:

- Obtain all sides of the story. Interview all parties involved in the dispute in private and ask open-ended questions.

- Maintain accurate records, and if possible record interviews so that they will be verbatim

- Maintain confidentiality, and do not reveal names of those involved.

- Preserve evidence wherever possible. When necessary, retain documents, copies of e-mails, phone records, etc. Obtain photographic evidence where applicable.

- Be sensitive to all parties involved, treating everyone with respect during interviews, especially when the matter is of a serious criminal matter.

- Report your findings without drawing conclusions.

Workplace investigations are an important external approach to resolving disputes in the workplace and insuring that all employees are treated fairly when a complaint is made. This investigation requires the investigator to be able to act swiftly and with a gentle approach within the employer, employees or union policies. It must be completed in good faith.

OVERVIEW:

Best Practices and Investigation Standards

It is important for those that work in the field to identify the regulator bodies that regulate private investigators or detectives, as well as companies that sell investigation services. This will allow you to determine the required qualifications, and courses needed to become licensed and potential employers in the State or Province that you work at. There are a number of associations that represent investigators in the United States and Canada.

It is standard practice to have a Code of Ethics and Privacy Policy available to corporate, civil, insurance, criminal clients and members of the public. These could be displayed on your website or provided to potential clients during the screening process. The staff at your company should be well aware of these policies.

All companies selling the services of private investigations should have a standard contract for clients to review and agree to the terms. This contract should be kept on file to identify the investigation details and its purpose.

Investigators should be aware of the agency policy for privacy, training and code of ethics within the organization. All employees should sign a confidentiality agreement, as well as, signed off that they have read all the manuals associated with the investigation company.

There are a number of other federal, provincial, state and municipal laws that investigators need to be aware of. The various laws will be outlined in the firm, company or agency policy manual for the investigators to review and keep a copy of.

Investigation Standards:

Intake of Investigation Assignment

- **Determine if Investigation is permissible by law** – depends on the laws of the state or province where the investigation is being conducted

- **Identification of client** and verification of client's reason to have the investigation conducted

- **Contract or agreement for investigation** - expectations of investigation company, statement of purpose of investigation and timeline for completion, rates and charges, retainer, penalties, confidentiality, budget, invoice and the end product that the client will receive - report, video, evidence etc.

- **Collection of information** from the client regarding the target of investigation.

- All investigators that investigate on behalf of an agency or firm will be fully aware of all policies related to the employer, signed an acknowledgement that they have read it and that the confidentiality will be maintained.

Organize leads and information

Files will be organized in a consistent manner:

- Client Information – name, address, contact info, company, investigation file name and reference number.
- Subject Information
  - Full name, address, telephone number, email address, nickname
  - Physical Description –age, gender, height, weight, hair color
  - Date of birth
  - Family status, partner, children, siblings, parents, roommates
- Subject Residence
  - Address
  - Type of dwelling – single, townhouse, two-story, etc.
  - Major intersection near subject's residence

- o Who owns the house?

- o Telephone listings shown at the residence

- Subject's vehicle – provided by the client

  - o Year, make, model, license plate number

  - o Ownership details if available

- Subject's Place of Employment

  - o Full company name, address, city

  - o Company contact information

  - o Position of subject at the company

  - o Methods of travel available for the subject, bus route, etc.

Possible related information on activity

  - o Any names and contact information of known family, friends, associates, or acquaintances

- Hobbies, sports, or membership in groups

Determining the Objectives of the Investigation:

- Establish the purpose of your investigation. The more specific you can be, the easier it will be to meet your objectives.

- Evaluate your objectives by asking yourself, "What do you need to know?"

- Identify the overall purpose of the investigation to be broken down into individual objectives either using a checklist of requirements or a plan of action to insure the most effective way to complete the investigation and meet the objective.

- Surveillance – schedule and determine number of days to stay within the budget

- Conduct inquiries and research where required

- Establish leads to determine if additional background inquiries is required.

Prepare the Investigation:

- Complete a background work up on the subject containing all relevant information to start the surveillance.

- Check information through public records, databases, etc.

- Establish a clear plan of action.

- Schedule investigation task according to the information confirmed about the subject.

- Summarize the objectives and the instructions and tasks for the investigator.

- Map the subject: complete an overview of locations that the subject might attend in the area of the residence, such as schools, malls and restaurants.

- Define the plan of the investigation tasks into a timeline in which to properly instruct the investigator and insure time management.

Conduct the Investigation Tasks list:

The nature of the investigation along with the objectives to be achieved will insure the use of one or more investigations tasks will be achieved.

- Surveillance
- Locate – witness, subject, claimant
- Inquiries/ Interviews/ Statements / Analysis
- Accident scene attendance – canvass for witnesses, photograph / video the scene, measure and survey and note any obstructions of views from various

angles/note any cameras in the area and
obtain video feed

- Search for data, records, or social media
for evidence

Investigators assigned to conduct tasks
should be qualified, experienced, or trained in the
area that they will be assigned. The assigned
investigator should familiarize themselves with the
information documented in the file and the
objectives of the investigation.

- Investigators should be knowledgeable of the
pertinent laws, regulations, acts, and other
legalities that govern private investigators or
detectives in the province or state or
federally.

- The investigator should be proficient in the
capabilities, use, proper care, and basic

maintenance of their equipment that will be utilized during the course of the investigation.

- The investigator should make notes of all investigation requirements and tasks at the earliest opportunity. Notes should be recorded in chronological order with the file name and number at the top of the page. A secondary heading that contains the date, location, weather, and investigator's name / license number should be recorded. All notes should be objective, record of facts, observations, and void of opinion.

- It is the investigators responsibility to maintain a record of time, mileage, expenses incurred on the investigation.

- The investigator shall also contact and keep the supervisor and / or client is informed of status and progress.

Assess Progress of the Investigation / Revaluate Objectives:

- Depending on the progress of the investigation, the facts and evidence discovered during the investigation process and dependent on results; it might be necessary to reevaluate objectives and find other methods of investigation. In these instances the investigation can be re-directed by the supervisor.

Reporting:

The information / evidence acquired during the investigation is reviewed and organized into an investigative report of findings that will be documented in hand written notes at the earliest time after the completion of each task.

- It is recommended the report commence with a brief opening summary or cover letter which reiterates the purpose of the investigation, a summary of the findings, brief explanation of any limitations.

- The report should include details regarding the subject, target, or incident being investigated. Including addresses, description, family status, photograph, and any other information discovered during the investigation.

- Summary of investigation tasks and results can also be provided.

- Detailed investigation notes / reports in chronological order that identifies the tasks that were conducted, date and time completed.

- If the investigation determined recommendations of further investigation that could be explored, if not listed or discussed in the intake or objectives; then such items can be included as further recommendations.

- The report should accompany any evidence items that might be required by the client – i.e. surveillance photos, video, written statements, public documents, and social media findings.

Security of Subject and File Information:

- All investigators should be familiar with the privacy laws in the state or province that the investigation is being conducted.

They should also know the federal laws that pertain to privacy.

- o All personal information should be stored in a secure location. If you keep personal information on your personal computer, it is important that you insure your computer is secure and no breach of privacy will occur.

- o If you have a file on the subject, all information should be handed back to your supervisor upon completion of the investigation. The agency will insure that the documents will be filed in a secured location at the office.

- If an investigator utilized a USB or other back up sources, once the file has been completed and handed into the office, it shall be deleted from this source to insure that no breach may occur.
- If a breach was to occur, you must notify your supervisor of the agency immediately so that the proper authorities can be notified of the breach.

Surveillance and video documentation:

- When conducting surveillance, an investigator should be aware that when obtaining video documentation of the focus should be on the subject of the investigation. The investigator will document his or her activities by zooming into this particular subject. The investigator should maintain focus on this subject and avoid obtaining video documentation of others in the area that are not related to the subject's activities.

- The evidence - the video tape / photographs should remain in a secure location and remain unaltered for the purpose of evidence in court.
- The investigator should be aware of the Evidence Act and the continuity of such evidence.

ORDER COPIES OF

FROM GUMSHOE TO

CYBER SLEUTH

TODAY!

_____COPIES @ 27.95 IN US= _____

_____COPIES @32.95 IN CANADA= _____

SUBTOTAL _____

US S&H FIRSTBOOK $3.50 _____

US S&H EACH BOOK THEREAFTER $1.00 EACH _____

CANADIAN POSTAGE APPLICABLE PER BOOK __$3. US
FUNDS_____

TOTAL _____

ORDERED BY:

_____

_____

ADDRESS:

_____

_____

CITY, STATE, ZIP _____

PHONE: (   ) _____

YOUR EMAIL ADDRESS: _____

FOR VOLUME ORDERS EXCEEDING 10 BOOKS, CONTACT:
AVEGASPUBLISHER@YAHOO.COM FOR SPECIAL PRICING

Make your cashier's check or money order payable to:

A Vegas Publisher, LLC

284C E. Lake Mead Parkway #262

Henderson, NV 89015

For Credit Cards or Pay Pal orders:

www.avegaspublisher.com

www.vegaspublisher.com

www.ingramcontent.com/pod-product-compliance
Lightning Source LLC
LaVergne TN
LVHW051458080426
835509LV00017B/1803